Black M

Black Critique

Series editors: Anthony Bogues and Bedour Alagraa

We live in a troubled world. The rise of authoritarianism marks the dominant current political order. The end of colonial empires did not inaugurate a more humane world; rather, the old order reasserted itself.

In opposition, throughout the twentieth century and until today, anti-racist, radical decolonization struggles attempted to create new forms of thought. Figures from Ida B. Wells to W.E.B. Du Bois and Steve Biko, from Claudia Jones to Walter Rodney and Amílcar Cabral produced work which drew from the historical experiences of Africa and the African diaspora. They drew inspiration from the Haitian revolution, radical black abolitionist thought and practice, and other currents that marked the contours of a black radical intellectual and political tradition.

The Black Critique series operates squarely within this tradition of ideas and political struggles. It includes books which foreground this rich and complex history. At a time when there is a deep desire for change, black radicalism is one of the most underexplored traditions that can drive emancipatory change today. This series highlights these critical ideas from anywhere in the black world, creating a new history of radical thought for our times.

Also available:

Black Minded

The Political Philosophy
of Malcolm X

Michael E. Sawyer

First published 2020 by Pluto Press
345 Archway Road, London N6 5AA

www.plutobooks.com

British Library Cataloguing in Publication Data
A catalogue record for this book is available from the British Library

ISBN   978 0 7453 4073 9   Hardback
ISBN   978 0 7453 4074 6   Paperback
ISBN   978 1 7868 0601 7   PDF eBook
ISBN   978 1 7868 0603 1   Kindle eBook
ISBN   978 1 7868 0602 4   EPUB eBook

This book is printed on paper suitable for recycling and made from fully
managed and sustained forest sources. Logging, pulping and manufacturing
processes are expected to conform to the environmental standards of the
country of origin.

Typeset by Stanford DTP Services, Northampton, England

Simultaneously printed in the United Kingdom and United States of America

Dedicated to my parents
Ernest and Theresa Sawyer

Contents

Acknowledgments

The most honest people to whom I mentioned that I was writing a book on Malcolm X asked, "what new thing could possibly be said about him?" It is only because of the unequivocal support of my dissertation chair, Professor Barrymore Anthony Bogues, that I had the confidence to imagine that this project might, in some small way, contribute to the work that has already so ably taken up the figure of Malcolm X and endeavor to say something "new," however incremental.

Throughout this process I have benefited from the unending support of friends and colleagues at Colorado College, most prominently, President Jill Tiefenthaler, Provost Alan Townsend, Dean of Students Mike Edmonds and Professor Jonathan Lee. During the latter stages of this project I was fortunate enough to be appointed Distinguished Visiting Professor of English and the Fine Arts at the United States Air Force Academy where I had the honor of teaching incredibly talented and intellectually curious cadets who asked probative and clarifying questions about the text in progress.

I owe a special type of gratitude to two members of "The Four Reprieved," Douglass "Too Short" Wilson and Awall "QueMonger" Gbadamosi, who checked on me every day in ways explicit and implied to ensure I brought this ship to shore. F.I.E.T.T.S.

My partner Dr Manya Whitaker makes all of this possible with her support and scholarly example.

My two college-student children have been helpful in ways it is hard to quantify. Ashley with her practical questions and Ellis (who shares a birthday with Malcolm X) for his encouragement.

Finally, none of this would be possible without my parents to whom this book is dedicated. This book is written from a place of love and I learned that from the place of peace and comfort they have always provided.

Introduction

"Many will ask what Harlem finds to honor this stormy, controversial and bold young captain – and we will smile."

Ossie Davis

This book came to be from a sudden awareness of my unconscious erasure of Malcolm X from the intellectual genealogy I was assembling to complete my dissertation in graduate school. The work of Frantz Fanon had driven me to graduate school and my studies focused on the complexity of W. E. B. Du Bois to the point that Malcolm X occurred to me, but never in the same way that I approached other thinkers. This is likely because the "thought" of Malcolm had been overcome by his acts. Or, perhaps more troubling, the speeches of this Black American just didn't seem to fit among the pantheon of philosophers, theorists, historians, writers and artists I was studying. As I was attempting to resolve a difficult section of writing, I had come across the iconic photo of H. Rap Brown with Stokely Carmichael and Amiri Baraka, *née* LeRoi Jones, and I decided to write to Rap, who is now known as Jamil Abdullah Al-Amin, in prison to get his take on what I was trying to pull together with respect to Fanon.

I included a large sample of the dissertation and a few weeks later I received a kind note from him; a week or so after that, he phoned. During one of our first conversations I raised the question of Fanon and his import to the intellectual tradition I was working through and Al-Amin stated the following:

El-Hajj Malik el-Shabazz is significant in that his example is the watermark of the struggles we experience over here. We're the only group on the planet that [sic] an African–American male, by the time he reaches 12 years old, has to make life and death decisions every time he leaves his home.[1]

I had not asked Al-Amin about Malcolm X in that my focus was on Fanon and I understood *Wretched of the Earth* to be the urtext for the radical political tradition that Al-Amin exemplifies. Jamil Al-Amin sped by the question of Fanon's thought and settled on what he called the "example," what I took to be something I have chosen to call "the embodied philosophy in motion of Malcolm X," as the critically import-ant touchstone for the ethical practice of radical politics. This caused me to realize that there was something that needed to be done in con-sidering the embodied praxis of radical politics by Malcolm X for its philosophical intentionality. Further, it required me to understand that privileging the written word or the pronouncement of specific philo-sophical or theoretical intent is not the limit of what can be considered "serious" philosophy. I was selling Malcolm X short in an effort to be considered a person who took up serious intellectual complexity: that was a profoundly irresponsible position. Malcolm X is obviously not the only example of this unconscious marginalization. I am aware that this goes, probably more poignantly, for feminist and queer thinkers who are also labeled as "activists," as if that moniker renders "philosopher" an impossibility. Malcolm X, among others, deserves better: the ambition of this book is to propose a different way to think about this life and its "example," in the parlance of Jamil Al-Amin.

The conversations with Al-Amin were generative for this text but what remained (and remains) unsaid between us is perhaps the most provoc-ative element of the manner in which the example of Malcolm X has framed the political praxis and life choices of an "absolute" radical like Jamil Abdullah Al-Amin. Readers may be familiar with the fact that Jamil is serving life in prison for the murder and attempted murder of police officers who he asserts were coming to murder him. He was convicted of the murder of one officer and the attempted murder of another after being taken into custody fleeing the state of Georgia. The question that I have *never* asked Al-Amin, in deference to censoring the nature of our correspondence to preserve his telephone privileges while imprisoned, is quite simply: how did he allow himself to be arrested relatively without incident, after a shootout with officers who were putatively trying to serve him with a warrant?

The answer to the question is of course one that has to come from Al-Amin and he, perhaps, may not have a clear response in that there are likely many circumstances surrounding both encounters that are difficult to keep track of, let alone assemble into a coherent, explanatory narrative. But isn't that the business of philosophy and theory? Endeav-oring to find abstract systems of understanding to establish a cause and effect relationship between thought and action? There is a way in which we can distill this concern down to the utility of social structures of oppression as, on one hand, recognized as legitimate, and on the other, useful for radical politics, for those engaged in projects of revolutionary alteration of ways of being. The question for Al-Amin would be: how did he allow himself to be taken into custody and held to account for an action that was literally designed to prevent him from being taken into custody, if we allow ourselves to take the police account as true?

The answer, in one sense, might be as simple as the desire to live under conditions of incarceration rather than to die in an attempt to avoid being locked up. That is satisfying in one register, but things are likely more complex and I will indulge my own ideas about how this works.

This seems to revolve around the "legitimacy" of a system that the person in question has spent years opposing as illegitimate. The question seems to be, and this paradox will haunt all of this consideration of the thought of Malcolm X, what elements of an illegitimate system might be employed in the practice of radical politics without doing violence to the project *in toto*. There is an example of this in the biography of Malcolm X that presents the same type of paradox that surrounds this unspoken element of my interaction with Jamil Al-Amin.

On February 9, 1965, Malcolm X tried to visit France but was denied entry into the nation by what he described as higher-ups in the French Foreign Ministry. Further, Malcolm X asserted at the time that he was certain that the French were acting upon the direction of the State Department of the United States. Both of these claims make sense. What I find difficult to understand is that Malcolm X further contends that the French authorities did not allow him to contact the US State Department to solve the problem. This is difficult to square with several of the foundational understandings that inform the political praxis of Malcolm X. He believes, axiomatically, that the United States government is corrupt and anti-Black by design. He believes that the corruption of the United States is born of a direct relationship to European imperialism. He believes that the United States government is intent upon assassinating him physically and ideologically. In spite of all of this, and in the face of understanding that the United States government, in coordination with the French government, have barred him from entering France, Malcolm X is frustrated by his inability to contact the State Department for redress. I understand this as a species of the same genus of subjective confusion as it relates to radical politics that seeks to develop practices that allow the subject to function within a hostile system of governance. This will be explored in detail in this text, but it should be marked as one of the primary questions that preoccupy this project: what of the materials of the state available to Malcolm's "so-called Negro" are useful for radical politics? Tracing this complex political project amounts to the creation of a literal *pharmakon*, poison, cure and scapegoat, by this philosophical endeavor. This understanding of the nature of the product of this philosophical system exposes the multiple layers of difficulty that face the work of Malcolm X and, in some sense, establish what can best be labeled as the *Idea of Malcolm X* versus the *Ideas of Malcolm X* that have represented the common way we access this figure. The purpose here is to examine the complexity of this political project and in some sense what I have come to label as the "Idea of Malcolm X" simultaneously.

Upon reflection, the "Idea" of Malcolm X, if not the details of his life, entered my consciousness as a very young child growing up on the far south side of Chicago during the 1970s and 1980s. Much of this was likely due to the omnipresence of the Nation of Islam (NoI) in the Black community during that time. Whatever deadly rift that existed between Malcolm X and the Nation was beyond my awareness; the members of the NoI that I encountered selling copies of the *Final Call* and bean pies on crowded corners in the summer were analogous to Malcolm X in my mind. I vividly recall being in the homes of Black people when I was a child and noting the almost ubiquitous presence of the calendar on the wall and I was always interested in what it meant for the household that marked the progress of time and planned future events beneath the placid image of Elijah Muhammad. Having no idea of the content of the politics of the Nation of Islam, I was profoundly aware of the structurally radical nature of their ambition for the Black community and understood Malcolm X to exemplify a type of Blackness that was oppositional to the popular understanding of Dr King, as the exemplar of the most ethical way forward.

It was not until I was in college, probably my second year, that I got my hands on *The Autobiography of Malcolm X: As Told to Alex Haley*.[2] The book remains one of three or four texts that I was literally unable to put down and, even with the flaws that have been revealed over the decades since its publication, it remains the first text I recommend to anyone who asks me what they should have on a list of books to help them to "understand" Black America.

It occurs to me, as I reflect on the complexity of attempting to account for the philosophical thought of Malcolm X, that there is a way in which the preoccupation with his biography extracts the robust philosophical content of his journey from our collective consciousness. What I mean is that the foundational concepts of something like the political philosophy of Malcolm X – economic and social justice, strident opposition to white supremacy, Black internationalism, etc. – finds itself hidden as the journey through that intellectual thicket is overwhelmed by the furious motion that attends his travels. This is at some distance from other important thinkers in the Black radical tradition who are known for their complex theoretical (if not philosophical) interventions, Frantz Fanon, in *my* thinking, being a prime example of this phenomenon. I have come to understand that my reading of the intellectual complexity of Fanon, or almost anyone else for that matter, is accomplished through the lens created by Malcolm X. I take this to be an improvisation on Ossie Davis' well-known eulogy of Malcolm, that I will quote here for its clarity.

Here – at this final hour, in this quiet place – Harlem has come to bid farewell to one of its brightest hopes – extinguished now, and gone from us forever. For Harlem is where he worked and where he struggled and fought – his home of homes, where his heart was, and where his people are – and it is, therefore, most fitting that we meet once again – in Harlem – to share these last moments with him. For Harlem has ever been gracious to those who have loved her, have fought her, and have defended her honor even to the death.

It is not in the memory of man that this beleaguered, unfortunate, but nonetheless proud community has found a braver, more gallant young champion than this Afro-American who lies before us – unconquered still. I say the word again, as he would want me to: Afro-American – Afro-American Malcolm, who was a master, was most meticulous in his use of words. Nobody knew better than he the power words have over minds of men. Malcolm had stopped being a "Negro" years ago. It had become too small, too puny, too weak a word for him. Malcolm was bigger than that. Malcolm had become an Afro-American and he wanted – so desperately – that we, that all his people, would become Afro-Americans too.

There are those who will consider it their duty, as friends of the Negro people, to tell us to revile him, to flee, even from the presence of his memory, to save ourselves by writing him out of the history of our turbulent times. Many will ask what Harlem finds to honor in this stormy, controversial and bold young captain – and we will smile. Many will say turn away – away from this man, for he is not a man but a demon, a monster, a subverter and an enemy of the black man – and we will smile. They will say that he is of hate – a fanatic, a racist – who can only bring evil to the cause for which you struggle! And we will answer and say to them: Did you ever talk to Brother Malcolm? Did you ever touch him, or have him smile at you? Did you ever really listen to him? Did he ever do a mean thing? Was he ever himself associated with violence or any public disturbance? For if you did you would know him. And if you knew him you would know why we must honor him.

Malcolm was our manhood, our living, black manhood! This was his meaning to his people. And, in honoring him, we honor the best in ourselves. Last year, from Africa, he wrote these words to a friend: "My journey", he says, "is almost ended, and I have a much broader scope than when I started out, which I believe will add new life and dimension to our struggle for freedom and honor and dignity in the States. I am writing these things so that you will know for a fact the tremendous sympathy and support we have among the African States for our Human Rights struggle. The main thing is that we keep a United Front wherein our most valuable time and energy will not be wasted fighting each other." However we may have differed with him – or with each other about him and his value as a man – let his going from us serve only to bring us together, now.

Consigning these mortal remains to earth, the common mother of all, secure in the knowledge that what we place in the ground is no more now a man – but a seed – which, after the winter of our discontent, will come forth again to meet us. And we will know him then for what he was and is – a Prince – our own black shining Prince! – who didn't hesitate to die, because he loved us so.[3]

I am preoccupied here with expanding our understanding of what Davis means by marking the "manhood" of Malcolm X, what he understands as "our living, black manhood." There is a way in which this can reductively be understood as a form of masculinity that can be regarded as problematic. I believe Davis and Malcolm X to be gesturing at something very different. One really need look no further than some of the trenchant critique from some quarters around the publication of Manning Marable's text, *Malcolm X: A Life of Reinvention*,[4] and a recent "revelation" about the personal life of Malcolm X and his wife, Betty Shabazz.

In the edited volume, *A Lie of Reinvention: Correcting Manning Marable's Malcolm X*,[5] the essay entitled "Malcolm X: What Measure of a Man? – Assessing the Personal Growth and Social Transformation of Malcolm X from an African-Centered Social Work Perspective," the author, Patricia Reid-Merritt, proposes the following:

> Marable's references to Malcolm X's sexual orientation *must be viewed as direct attacks on Malcolm's manhood* [my italics], which Marable believed the Black community had embraced as the ultimate symbol of the strong, masculine, defiant image of a Black man. For example, when offering insights to Malcolm's supposedly secret sex life, Marable writes the following: "Based on circumstantial but strong evidence, Malcolm was probably describing his own homosexual encounters ..."

Several things present themselves here beyond the question of the historical methodology proposed by Reid-Merritt that revolves around the notion of a reductive understanding of "manhood" that I believe is contra to what Davis means in his eulogy. What I mean is that sexual orientation and "manhood" are not related concepts. To the extent that the work of Malcolm X might be marginalized because someone thinks he might have been queer is disappointing at best, and at worst begins to define the notion of toxic masculinity, Black or otherwise. Stated simply, the reason one might be deemed lacking with respect to representing "strong, masculine, [and] defiant" Black manhood could only have to do with sexual orientation, which empirically it does not. The same is exemplified by a recently-auctioned letter from Malcolm X to Elijah Muhammad:

> In the 1959 typed note, up for sale for $95,000 at MomentsInTime. com, X writes to his mentor, Nation of Islam leader Elijah Muhammad, that his wife, Betty Shabazz, had complained that he had "never given her any real satisfaction" and "said to me that if I didn't watch out she was going to embarrass me and herself'" (which under questioning she later said she was going to seek satisfaction elsewhere).

The letter goes into detail about the problems between X and Shabazz.

> The main source of our troubles was based upon SEX. She placed a great deal more stress upon it than I was physically capable of doing. One day, she told me that we were incompatible sexually because I had never given her any real satisfaction ... [She] outright told me that I was impotent ... and I was like an old man (not able to engage in the act long enough to satisfy her) ... Her remarks like this were very heartbreaking to me.[6]

In this instance, the fact that someone would be willing to spend $95,000 to assemble archival "proof" of the insufficiency of Malcolm X's manhood speaks to another form of reductive masculinity that depends upon sexuality.

I do not understand the formulation by Davis to be this type of sexually-charged notion of manhood but rather to be a type of radical intellectualism that is grounded in what we can understand as "Black-Humanhood." The manner in which this thinking endeavored to do so is, in many ways, the plot of this story, but here in the Introduction we should pause and consider the "Negro."

The term "Negro," specifically, Malcolm X's modification of the term to "the 'so-called' Negro," will appear repeatedly in this book in order for us to demarcate the boundaries of the Negro, the notion of what he means by "so-called" and how that recedes into the more appropriate understanding of African–American to mark the complexity of the subject in question. As Ossie Davis proposed, this is a mind-set. To exceed the boundaries of the imposition of the marginalized subjectivity of the Negro, Malcolm X embarks on a complex intellectual project that I suggest is best labeled by his own framework, Black Minded.

In reviewing Malcolm X's public statements, the notion of being "Black Minded" appears in only two instances of which I am aware. The first time the concept appears is in response to a question from the audience on July 5, 1964 at the second Organization of African Unity (OAAU) rally and then, more formally, on January 7, 1965, in his speech "Prospects for Freedom in 1965." Unlike many other concepts Malcolm X presents during the various public forums in which he presented his ideas (speeches, interviews, debates and responses to questions from the public), he does not unpack what he means by "Black Minded" and it is framed here as more than the title for this text but rather the overriding goal and structure of his thinking. What I mean here by "goal" is to understand being Black Minded as a thought experiment that recaptures Blackness as an intellectual project for the purpose of restructuring the "so-called Negro" into what Malcolm understands as the Afro-American that I will attempt to reveal here as a complex, transnational form of radical political subjectivity.

The idea first appears during the question and answer period after the second OAAU rally, when Malcolm X has the following dialog with a member of the audience:

> *Questioner*: You once stated that the only solution for the "so-called" Negro was ultimately to return to Africa. Then at the last meeting, you said we should turn to Africa culturally and spiritually, but politically should stay in this country.[7]

This question/statement succinctly articulates the core problem confronted by Malcolm X as a political thinker (who I intend to examine by employing the academic discipline of political philosophy) and as himself a unique philosopher who spends much of his short adult life in a complex struggle with the core principles informing this individual's question: *How do displaced political subjects who are politically and economically marginalized members of a societal order establish themselves as sovereign actors without forming a completely separate and self-authorized system of governance?* Malcolm X answers the question with the following statement that exposes an evolution in his thinking on this foundational problematic:

> *Malcolm*: Hold it right there. The first statement that I made, I made before going to Africa myself. I spent about five weeks over there speaking to every kind of African leader that I could gain access to. And the net result of that trip was that if our people go, they're welcome. *But those who are politically mature over there say that we would be wise to play a role at this time right* here [my italics].[8]

This discussion illustrates important elements of the intellectual project pursued by Malcolm X: first, he is open to the possibility of altering fundamental elements of his thinking and second, that alteration is based upon a phenomenological experience that is processed through the lens of particular epistemological predilections. This interaction is a primary exemplar of what I have labeled as the philosophical practice of Malcolm X that is identifiable by this "Thinking in Motion."

It is important here to pause and clearly set up the way in which I am proposing that "Black Minded" is both an epistemological tendency and a radical political subjectivity.

Stated succinctly, Black Minded is a way of knowing about the self and, in so doing, understanding the self to be a necessarily radical political subject as the threshold condition of that knowing. What that means, in this instance, is that in spite of the negative framework of white supremacy that reinforces the existence of Blackness as a wholly negative way of being, to navigate that labyrinth to find what Malcolm X proposes as a form of objective truth, is radically to reestablish the political existence of a subject that is, in this context, only political. Specifically, Blackness in the form of radically political/aware Black Mindedness is a political claim that, in its enunciation, is a cry for true subjectivity in the form of Being Human.

Returning to the discussion, the conversation moves forward through Malcolm providing his interlocutor with the current state of his thinking on the matter. The questioner is somehow dissatisfied with the answer he has received and asks a follow-up that is lost to distortion on the recording, but we have access to Malcolm X's answer that in fact poses several questions of his own as elements of the response.

> *Malcolm*: Brother, if all of us wanted to go back to Africa – you wouldn't be satisfied to go back all by yourself, I know that. Your desire would be to see all of us go back if I am judging you correctly. Then how would you create a situation, number one, *that would make all of us black-minded enough to want to go back* [my italics], or make all of us have a thorough enough knowledge of what it is like over there to want to go back, or make this man so fed up with us he'd want to send us there?[9]

Malcolm X presents a series of options that would serve to satisfy his interlocutor's desire to facilitate a separation of people of African descent from conditions of oppression in the United States by returning to Africa. The first of these is the notion of being *"Black Minded" enough* to desire separation, which I am reading as the most desirable (in the thinking of Malcolm X) of the options he proposes, which include a knowledge base that draws people of African descent to Africa or, finally, a way of being in the United States that becomes so disruptive of societal order that Black people find themselves expelled from the nation.

The notion of being or becoming *sufficiently* Black Minded recurs several months later, as referenced above, and in an arguably more disciplined fashion in that it is part of the prepared remarks delivered by Malcolm X in the speech we know by the title "Prospects of Freedom." Here he proposes the following:

> It is only when the nationalist-minded or *black-minded* [my italics] Afro-American goes abroad to the African continent and establishes direct lines of communication and lets the African brothers know what is happening over here, and know that our people are not so dumb that we are blind to our true condition and position in this structure, that the Africans begin to understand us and identify with us and sympathize with our problems, to the point where we are willing to make whatever sacrifices are necessary to see that their long-lost brothers get a better break than we have been getting up to now.[10]

Malcolm establishes an analogous relationship between nationalism (Black Nationalism) and the notion of being Black Minded. There is a possible reading of this formulation that views this as two distinct paths to the same goal: Nationalism or Black Minded. I would argue that these are substantively overlapping concepts that, at this stage of the evolutionary nature of this thinking, are synonyms that illustrate the fact of this "Thinking in Motion," that Malcolm X employs to get at what he frames as the goal of his theory and praxis which is "... freedom, justice, [and] equality."[11] Malcolm X understands these goals as the necessary correction to a social context of broad-based oppression that he frames as suffering based upon "political oppression at the hands of the white man, economic exploitation at the hands of the white man, and social degradation at the hands of the white man."[12] The political, the economic, and the social represent the trilateral concerns of Malcolm X's thinking and what this text intends to address is the manner in which the metaphysical notion of "Being" or "Becoming" sufficiently "Black Minded" serves to provide the tools for satisfying the political, economic and social concerns of Malcolm X, who elaborates a complex understanding of a "nationalist" project.

It is important to be aware of the manner in which the unique understanding of what is meant by Black Nationalism by Malcolm X is situated here within the broad cultural phenomenon of Black Liberation that ranges from something like the integrationist goals of the civil rights movement to projects of nationalism as diverse as the Black Consciousness movement in South Africa to Black separatists in the United States and, of course, Pan-Africanist thought. George Fredrickson's text, *Black Liberation: A Comparative History of Black Ideologies in the United States and South Africa*, provides an entry into establishing these distinctions that relies upon Malcolm X as the embodied exemplar of an alteration in Black Nationalist thought. Fredrickson writes:

> This repudiation of a strictly genetic view of blackness paralleled a subtle and little noticed difference between African–American nationalism of the 1960s and the earlier varieties associated with Edward Blyden, Alexander Crummel, and Marcus Garvey. As we have seen, these forerunners were men of dark complexions who distrusted mullatoes and at times openly disparaged them. But in the 1960s, the foremost champion of blackness could be the light-skinned and red-haired Malcolm X. The implicit message was that one was as black as one felt, and that people of African ancestry who retained the integrationist view that white culture was superior to black culture continued to be "Negroes" rather than "blacks", however dark complexioned they happened to be …Whether or not the new American affirmation of a non-genetic blackness influenced the racial thinking of Black Consciousness, there can be no doubt that both movements innovated significantly in making race consciousness more a matter of existential choice and political awareness than of biological determination.
>
> Another way that Black Consciousness departed from Pan-Africanist precedent and drew closer to American black nationalism of the 1960s was its emphasis on psychological rehabilitation as a precondition of political resistance.[13]

This notion of how to understand Malcolm X's employment of nationalism as a political ideology will be a recurring problem in this text in that it serves, in many ways, as the *telos* of his thinking. But here, the important matter of existentialism as the central thematic of the embodied notion of a broadly-defined "Blackness" is foundational to the intellectual innovation of Malcolm X's philosophical system and the reason the detailed analysis here begins with ontology.

The ground covered here in this opening section exposes the complexity of addressing Malcolm X as a political philosopher in the sense we understand that term both academically and colloquially. The academic notion of political philosophy is a complicated matter yet one that has a canon of academic writing that allows a point of entry for debate. The colloquial is more complex and deals first with the white supremacist notion that Black people are incapable of rational thought generally and philosophical thought specifically. Unlike most "philosophers" who represent the canon of the Western tradition, Malcolm X has left very little in written form. The exercise of establishing a corpus for purposes of analysis requires that his dynamic discourse be employed as the archive. The fact of the lack of the typical written documentation that attends the examination of philosophy is one thing when the Western mind confronts the notion that Socrates never "wrote" anything and quite another under the imposed subaltern notion that the absence of writing on the part of Black minds is predictable in that the Black is assumed to be resistant to learning and rationality. What this seems to mean is that there is a binary performance of the "lack" that is the condition of Blackness as a construct of white supremacy that says that there is no possibility of these subjects creating something like philosophical thought and that, furthermore, the search for the existence of this thought by Black academics is a kind of quixotic alchemy designed to resurrect something like Black thought from the fact of its manifest absence.

In order to establish a point of departure for this intellectual exercise it is important to make an argument for understanding Malcolm X as an activist as well as a practitioner of a particular brand of radical political philosophy. While practicing a form of radical politics, he also presents an epistemological predisposition that allows for the malleability of his philosophical framework, theoretical approach and praxis within parameters that privilege the goal rather than the methodology for success. This malleability is meant to accompany the notion of Malcolm X and his "Thinking in Motion" and to analogize his intellectual project to a quest that is encumbered by unknown obstacles. The goal of his journey is firmly in mind and Malcolm X is constantly and unapologetically choosing the most advantageous mode of "travel" to reach it. This is in some sense a methodological point that requires an equally "malleable" set of analytic tools for the study of this brand of political thought and what I am situating as the "always/already" radical nature of something like Black political thought. In this realm, thinking about the self in a way that elides the traps laid by white supremacist epistemologies, is to recognize the political nature of humanity that is the threshold condition of fracturing the way in which Blackness is only witnessed as a political way of being that must necessarily be a lack, since that is its positionality in that system of logic. Radical Blackness, Black Minded being, is necessarily a recognition and refutation of the political at the same moment it opens a space for the human to emerge as a subject with the potentiality of positive political existence versus an existence that is only real in its irrefutable marginality through politics. Much as "Peanut Butter and Jelly Sandwich" does not require a set of directions to produce or recognize its existence. Within the logic of white supremacy, to be Black is to be marginalized. Within the philosophical system of Malcolm X, "Black Minded" is both recipe and a description of the thing itself.

An example of this malleability is illustrated in an examination of the complex relationship between Malcolm X and the Nation of Islam. There has justifiably been a great deal of effort invested in examining this fractured relationship. There is, however, a way in which this focus tends to damage our ability to discern foundational elements of his system of thinking. The break with the Nation is empirically a fact, but the reasons for and the implications of that perceived breach in Malcolm X's faith in the Black Muslim Movement generally, and the message of Elijah Muhammad specifically, are framed here as a predictable abandonment of a way of thinking that had lost its utility for progress toward his goal. Malcolm X did not allow the divine imperative of faith to override the need to progress toward his goal to develop a practical program for the political, economic and social equality of people of African descent, and perhaps an evolving understanding of the ills of patriarchy in radical political movements. Stated differently, the purported divinity of Elijah Muhammad as the "Messenger of Allah" was of perhaps secondary or even tertiary importance when measured against Malcolm X's fundamental project. Probing this thinking is not meant to argue that Malcolm X was not ensnared, positively or negatively, by potentially debilitating forms of intellectual purity that are represented by blind religious faith. Rather, the point is to propose that an examination of his thinking benefits from establishing his "first philosophy," which is goal-related rather than epistemological. This allows one to witness the evolutionary nature of Malcolm X's thought in a different register that represents the foundation of his philosophical practice. By foregrounding the goal of his political philosophy rather than the discreet elements of his intellectual framework, one can witness the logic of the eclectic jettisoning of systems of thought that can be misunderstood as primary.

Introductory remarks in Malcolm X's April 3, 1964 speech, known as "The Ballot or the Bullet," where he explicitly references his religion as being secondary to considerations of political praxis toward a project of political viability for Black people, buttresses the argument for this reading practice. On this point he is explicit:

> Although I'm still a Muslim, I'm not here tonight to discuss my religion. I'm not here to try and change your religion. I'm not here to argue or discuss anything that we differ about, because it's time for us to submerge our differences and realize that it is best for us to first see that we have the same problem, a common problem ...[14]

What I am gesturing to here, in very preliminary fashion, in order to unpack this proposition in some detail, is that there is a predisposition in the political thinking of Malcolm X that rendered his religion, which at the outset seemed to be the primary driving force behind his political and social resurrection, as a tool rather than a means in and of itself. The Nation of Islam, or Islam more generally, appears to exist for Malcolm X as a vehicle toward a project of radical humanism in the face of subject-deforming forces of oppression. This means that religious practice for Malcolm X must serve to ameliorate real conditions of oppression rather than serve as a means to blunt the effects of subjugation through palliative faith. This, at least in the mind of Malcolm X, is a critical difference between his political philosophy and its relationship to religion and the normative understanding of Christian-based movements that privilege civil rights.

The same goes for his understanding of the utility of arrest as a form of spectacle as opposed to the quotidian and oftentimes invisible machinations of the carceral state. All of these elements of the thinking of Malcolm X are arguably present in his biography. One can readily see the layers of complication that appear as soon as one begins to examine Malcolm X's thinking, in that his biographical details always threaten to overwhelm the analysis of the thinking that is at least companion to if not causal of these events. This is not an argument to refute or dismiss the efficacy of biographical projects generally, or biographical projects focused on Malcolm X specifically. The debt this project owes to the existence of the canonical 1964 autobiography by Alex Haley, that in many ways and for many years stood alone as a point of access to Malcolm X outside of recordings of his speeches, cannot be over-stated. As previously mentioned, the publication of historian Manning Marable's study, *Malcolm X: A Life of Reinvention*, introduced a revitalized and controversy-plagued series of engagements with the life of Malcolm X and in many ways presents a scaffold that informs the direction of this book. Marable, as indicated by the tagline of his text, focused on the transitional elements of Malcolm's biography that pick up, in great detail, shifts like the one from the Nation of Islam to the formation of his Muslim Mosque, Incorporated and the Organization of African American Unity.

The desired contribution of this effort is framed as both an intellectual genealogy that will endeavor to unearth explicit and implicit influences as well as an effort to expose, in some detail, the contours of what I am labeling as a political philosophy on the part of Malcolm X that might broadly be defined as a form of revolutionary politics that is specific to the plight of people of African descent in the United States. This thinking draws on the era of anti-colonial movements and formative post-colonial philosophy and represents an essential pillar in an edifice of Africana philosophy that is effectively, if not consciously, bracketed by the thinking of W. E. B. Du Bois and that of Frantz Fanon. These figures, Du Bois and Fanon, in contradistinction to the approach that preoccupies our analysis of Malcolm X, are primarily discussed in terms of their written intellectual production rather than the contours of their biography. I hope to privilege the intellectual production, context and influences on Malcolm X in order to be in a position to marry these approaches for a richer understanding of this important figure.

This requires a multidimensional methodological approach to assembling this intellectual mosaic for the purposes of coherent examination. This will be an exercise in hermeneutics that is decentered from its traditional methodological moorings in that, as mentioned above, there is very little of the carefully-formed written word that typically serves as the stuff of philosophical analysis. This hermeneutic exercise cannot be separated from the fact that it is often a product of discourse on the part of Malcolm X with interlocutors ranging from friendly audiences to hostile members of the press bent on establishing his thought as both radical and idiosyncratic. There is something categorically different about thinkers developing concepts under the klieg lights of the media as opposed to the strictures of a carefully-edited writing project. Epistemology will be important here: how does Malcolm X know what he knows? Or, perhaps more to the point, what is it about the subject in question that renders him susceptible to various forms of philosophical thought that serve as the point of departure for his own intellectual particularity? In spite of this mélange of disciplinary approaches, the polyglot nature of Malcolm's political philosophy can only be examined in terms of the intellectual phenomenon under consideration: there is an argument/requirement, from an academic perspective, to offer a label for what is being examined.

This requires that we first understand the way Malcolm X situates philosophy as an intellectual tool for the accomplishment of political goals. On December 20, 1964, at the Audubon Ballroom, Malcolm X articulated his understanding of philosophy as a tool for political reformation or revolution. He states the following:

> This is the type of philosophy that we want to express among our people. We don't need to give them a program, not yet. First, give them something to think about. If we give them something to think about and start them thinking in a way that they should think, they'll see through all this camouflage that's going on right now. It's just a show – the result of a script written for somebody else. The people will take that script and tear it up and write one for themselves. And you can bet that when you write the script for yourself, you're always doing something different than you'd be doing if you followed somebody else's script.[15]

Here Malcolm X articulates a broad claim regarding one of the most complex problems confronting projects of radical societal change: sequentiality. Here, the proposal seems to be that practical political programs become *effect* to the *cause* of an alteration in the thinking of the subjects in question. What that means for Malcolm X, as articulated in the quote here, is that the programs that are the product of these altered thought processes will necessarily speak to the project of radical societal change. This does not eliminate the possibility of elements of the context of living that caused the political tension in the first place to remain in place, in that the alteration of the intellectual position of subjects would necessarily alter the implication of any type of action.

Stated differently, the content of any activity, for Malcolm X, seems to be understood with respect to its political efficacy and how it relates to the form of political thought in which it is "contained." Further, Malcolm X requires here that political activity or, perhaps more carefully considered, structural elements of political systems be identified as what they actually represent, and have whatever "camouflage" that exists removed. The statement under examination here leaves a great deal of latitude for divining what Malcolm X might mean with this formulation.

He has a well-documented level of disdain for the theory and practice of the civil rights movement generally and there is a way in which one might imagine that he is concerned with both this political praxis and its reliance upon the letter of the US Constitution. This line of reasoning on the part of Malcolm X is foundational to what might be characterized as Black political theology as the label for the philosophical practice with the understanding that it has critically important points of departure from the Christianity that informed the core of the civil rights movement. The core principle here is that institutions, religion included, have several registers of utility; properly employed, they can be useful for projects of political radicalism.

This text is self-consciously resistant to being distracted by the important "Martin vs. Malcolm" debate and in many ways is informed by the iconic ending of Spike Lee's *Do the Right Thing*, with a crawl that begins with a quote from Martin Luther King:

> Violence as a way of achieving racial justice is both impractical and immoral. It is impractical because it is a descending spiral ending in destruction for all. The old law of an eye for an eye leaves everybody blind. It is immoral because it seeks to humiliate the opponent rather than win his understanding; it seeks to annihilate rather than to convert. Violence is immoral because it thrives on hatred rather than love. It destroys community and makes brotherhood impossible. It leaves society in monologue rather than dialogue. Violence ends by defeating itself. It creates bitterness in the survivors and brutality in the destroyers.[16]

This is followed by a quote from Malcolm X:

> I think there are plenty of good people in America, but there are also plenty of bad people in America and the bad ones are the ones who

seem to have all the power and be in these positions to block things that you and I need. Because this is the situation, you and I have to preserve the right to do what is necessary to bring an end to that situation, and it doesn't mean that I advocate violence, but at the same time I am not against using violence in self-defense. I don't even call it violence when it's self-defense, I call it intelligence.[17]

That can reductively be understood to represent oppositional views, except that the two speakers are talking about two different things. In the same film this is exemplified by the character Smiley, who is engaged in peddling pictures of the image of Malcolm X and Martin Luther King smiling and shaking hands that eschews the conceptualization of radical opposition but asserts, visually, that there is a common space between these thinkers who are invested in addressing different aspects of the coercive structure of white supremacy. In the quotes that close *Do the Right Thing*, King is addressing violence as a means of achieving racial justice versus what Malcolm X understands as a tool of self-protection. Where they meet in the middle, as in the photo being sold by Smiley, reveals a common understanding that racial justice, as an abstract concept, tends to provide the type of self-protection, broadly understood, that Malcolm X has as his concern. What differentiates the two thinkers is the existing structure of the American Democratic Project that King believes can accommodate the presence of Black people, and that Malcolm X finds to be wholly insufficient. With that understanding, the discursive presence of violence and its relationship to state-making is predictably absent from the thought of King and necessary (more on this later) in that of Malcolm X. With that understanding, I feel comfortable avoiding the debate over the efficacy of the disparate understandings of the utility of the structures of America for the subjective revitalization of the diasporic Black person and intend to focus on the implication of Malcolm's logic, which believes there are elements of the project that may prove useful in its destruction. The "difference" between the two thinkers is only marginally "methodological" with respect to the employment of violence. Malcolm X simply does not understand the notion of self-defense to be related to racial justice as defined by King. The tension here is how one understands the project of achieving justice and whether the foundational notion of security in the body is, in some sense, a foundational aspect of human-ness or something authorized and secured by the state. Further, whether the tools of the state in question can service projects of radical societal change.

This facilitates an understanding of how a fundamental tool of Western democracy, the vote, which has been employed to marginalize African–Americans, can somehow be a central component of a project for dismantling the conditions of subjugation. This complexity is best served by the important meditation on this phenomenon by Audre Lorde in the canonical essay, "The Master's Tools Will Never Dismantle the Master's House." Lorde asks:

> What does it mean when the tools of racist patriarchy are used to examine the fruit of that same patriarchy? It means that only the most narrow perimeters of change are possible and allowable.[18]

This gestures at an important element of Malcolm X's thought that must be confronted in comprehensive fashion in two ways: patriarchy and forms of male entitlement. First, whether the assemblage of cultural and political institutions that confound the political, social and economic viability of Black people, which are the product of patriarchal white supremacy, can be employed to dismantle themselves, and second, whether Black feminist epistemologies might serve as a positive corrective to the thinking of Malcolm X that may be implicated in the worst forms of misogyny. This effort will endeavor to understand the proposal by Malcolm X that speaks to Lorde here through his notion that the tools of white supremacy can prove useful in radical projects. The prospect for results here may prove to be negatively related to his own inability to grapple with the limitations of foundational notions of male imperative in the world of politics. It would be reductive, in my mind, to propose that Malcolm X is anti-woman or anti-feminist, but it is critically important to understand how his investment in the subservience of women to men and the need to demonstrate both manhood and political viability through the protection of women must be interrogated. This thinking operates in multiple vectors, but the one that seems most obvious is to examine how patriarchy (broadly understood) operates in the thinking of Malcolm X and further to think carefully about how a philosophical system that is implicated by that framework may have devastating flaws for developing an egalitarian system of radical politics. What this means is that to tend to the radical potentiality of Black Mindedness requires attention to its original formulaic patriarchy. Revisiting Lorde, the question would frame itself as something like: What does it mean when ideologies that are invested in forms of patriarchy are employed to address the needs of politically marginalized peoples, without dealing with the imperatives of gender or sexuality? As a practical matter, the reasoning and motivation behind a project taking up the thinking of Malcolm X has, as a component of its intellectual fodder, the question of the efficacy of his project in the contemporary moment. To evaluate this discourse from the perspective of its life beyond its "time" one must query whether it is possible for it to have utility in evolved notions of radical politics that push against "maleness" as first philosophy and exemplar of political viability. Much more will be said on this complex aspect of Malcolm X's thinking in several places in this narrative.

With this caveat, the notion of employing the discipline of philosophy to examine the thought of Malcolm X requires one to question whether the method matches the subject under examination. To propose axiomatically that Malcolm X is a "political philosopher" is, at its outset, to resolve a debate that first complicates the lines of demarcation between philosophy and theory and in this case pushes further into the question of social activism versus a practice of philosophy or theory. Further, the question of excavating thinkers of African descent from their exile from the world of "philosophy" is fundamentally to confront the presupposition of the inferiority of Black people that renders them incapable of philosophical thought and positive political existence. These questions are best dealt with here before launching into an argument that situates Malcolm X as a political philosopher in thought and practice, because we must first resolve what can be framed as a foundational methodological concern, that being defining the practice of Africana political philosophy.

Generally, Leo Strauss's *What is Political Philosophy? And Other Studies* proposes the following:

> Philosophy is essentially not possession of the truth, but quest for the truth ... Of philosophy thus understood, political philosophy is a branch. Political philosophy will then be an attempt to replace opinion about the nature of political things by knowledge of the nature of political things ... Political philosophy ought to be distinguished from political thought in general. By political thought we understand the reflection on, or the exposition of, political ideas ... Hence, all

political philosophy is political thought but not all political thought is political philosophy.[19]

The particularity of the "political things" that confront the subject engaged in the practice of Africana political philosophy requires a necessary expansion of the parameters of political philosophy articulated by Strauss. Further, the question of the relationship, or perhaps even the "possibility" of something like a philosophical practice on the part of Black people is given careful examination by Fred Moten in his essay "There Is No Racism Intended" in his text *The Universal Machine*. Here, Moten is pressing on the legacy of Emmanuel Levinas as a thinker who has a reputation, even within Black thought, as a member of the group of thinkers understood by Paul Gilroy as those who "have been bold enough … to approach the metaphysical potency of racism …"[20] This collection of thinkers, "[a]ccording to Gilroy … includes W. E. B. Du Bois, Mahatma Gandhi, Eric Voegelin, Jean-Paul Sartre, Frantz Fanon, Michel Foucault, and Giorgio Agamben,"[21] along with Levinas. The principal concern explored by Moten is the assertion by Levinas of the primacy of European modes of thought with respect to philosophy. The import of that thinking for this analysis is again to wonder how the non-European "philosopher" finds a space of recognition within a discourse that Levinas asserts is about the fact that "for [him] European man is central, in spite of all that has happened to us during this century, in spite of 'the savage mind.'"[22] For Moten this opens a line of questioning that destabilizes the utility of the thinking of Levinas in the manner in which Gilroy understands its productivity in matters of race. For the thinking explored here, the question that immediately presents itself revolves around the "possibility" of what Levinas understands as philosophy and its dedication to the restoration and maintenance of the European mode of thinking meant to mark the savage mind as irretrievably so and at the same time abandoning the notion of the centrality of European man. In short, following Levinas, thinking that is designed to accomplish these goals is necessarily anti-philosophical in its anti-European situatedness.

For a thinker like Malcolm X, there is absolutely no confusion about the true nature of the "political things" that he confronts in assembling a political philosophy that exists to undermine the goals of both Strauss and Levinas. As I mentioned earlier, the question for Africana philosophy, a necessarily oppositional intellectual practice, is two-fold: how to dismantle the political structures that are designed to marginalize the subject in question and next how to develop, almost simultaneously, an alternative political structure that facilitates the continued existence of the formally marginalized subject. If we axiomatically accept the notion that the Cartesian *cogito* forms the foundation of philosophical examination of the self in the Western tradition, there is an important complication at the outset that necessarily situates Africana political philosophy at a remove from the discipline under consideration by Strauss. Further, and here is where the thinking of Levinas suggests a type of implicit if not explicit racism, to the extent that the practice of philosophy is understood to be in support of the establishment of European man as exemplary, the possibility of a philosophy in opposition to that task is impossible. In the sense that Strauss struggles to identify a specific task for philosophy, Levinas does not, and it is this breach that requires the philosophical tradition under examination here to establish new ways of thinking in order to survive.

Stated simply, the explicit task here is to consider how a body that has been layered in abjection or negatively framed – *Blackness* – can serve as the locus of a positive political project that is fueled by robust political thought or philosophical reflection on "truth."

I believe that Malcolm X begins his philosophical practice from a complex understanding of the *cogito* as it relates to the Black bodies in question and in refutation of Levinas. These bodies have been conditioned, through coercion, to consider the self and find the self to be in a condition of *lack* and in this deficit to find something that can best be labeled self-hatred: *I think therefore I hate myself*. The struggle here at the opening moments of a political philosophical project on the part of people of African descent is first to distance the self from the politically-formed nature of the self in order to achieve a measure of separation from the unity of mind and body that is the result of the political formation of the Negro. Therefore, distorting Strauss through Malcolm X, I would alter his question to: *What is Africana political philosophy?* And answer it by asserting that politics as such, or perhaps what Strauss would call political thought/theory, is marking the lived experience of the body as it functions within a discernible social order. Africana political philosophy, again distorting Strauss through Malcolm X, is the structuring of a body of thinking that establishes a political order that allows it to experience the world in a manner that, in turn, facilitates the erasure of the conflict-based relationship between the body and the consciousness that inhabits it. Further, and this is in terms of destabilizing Levinas, the task at hand is nothing if not complete refutation of the notion of the centrality of European man.

Leaving aside for the moment the explicit assertion with which I began, which proposes a hostility between body and mind as the "thing" in Malcolm's thinking, I wonder if the body, as a particular type of receptor, is operative here in this thinking. Basically the body is a type of political "nerve-ending" that is then in communication with the intellect and consciousness in important ways that generate a certain type of truth that forces the *Malcolm X-ian* consciousness to ask questions that are at the behest of his body. There will be more on this in the discussion on the embodied nature of this thinking later, but I am endeavoring to mark the import of dealing with the *cogito* as the foundation of Western philosophical practice as implicated in that same system of thought's creation of the Negro. The question that remains is what are the implications of Africana thought or, stated more carefully, what are the points of contact and separation between the Western-centered notion of philosophy and thought, and coding these for the purposes of the experience of the racialized other. Lewis Gordon, in his *Existentia Africana*, takes up this distance from the norm that is represented by the distorted relationship between the mind and body. Gordon writes that "[a]n adult black who is well adjusted is an 'abnormal black.' An adult black who is not well adjusted is a 'normal black,' which ironically means an 'abnormal person,' or simply an 'abnormality.'"[23]

What is important here is that the questioning of the "body" becomes a prime motivator for the thinking of Malcolm X in that he is preoccupied with the relationship of the Black body to its need to take responsibility for itself through a product of positive awareness, based, at the outset, on the process of (re)naming. What Malcolm X seems to be asking is what the Africana mind needs to change about either itself, its perceptions of self, or its relationship to its body in order to effect a resolution of this question of normal versus abnormal. What follows this effort is the analytic dimension of Black versus white in order to achieve a point of departure for projects of radical political achievement? Is it valid to seek to reorient the body in certain kinds of ways, real or imagined, that tend to mitigate or perhaps eradicate the question of hatred of the self? Might the project of reordering society as a whole lead to an alternative or a wholly new way of being with the body? "I am inside someone who loves me ..." would be the most obvious change inaugurated by this thinking.

It seems to me that returning to the argument made by Strauss above, one might productively label the first of these options a type of lived experience that is a way of being within an established order that could be labeled political thought/theory. The second, the notion of altering the social order *tout court*, would be considered a philosophical project or a set of concerns that deal with establishing a framework for what amounts to truth by reordering the terms of the truth rather than the performance of a type of being within structures of normativity.

The foundation for thinking of Malcolm X as a "political philosopher" is based upon the requirement for Malcolm to achieve the goal of establishing a sovereign way of political life for formerly marginalized people within the political structure that is the author and support for their continued marginalization. This is the complexity of nationalism without sovereign geographic spatiality that is protected by its own self-referential autonomy that is recognized as being external to its borders. What I mean here is that, at the most basic level, Malcolm X is a political philosopher in substance based upon this question of structuring a form of nationalism that resists the normative understanding of what it means to construct and become a member of a state, post-Westphalia.

Malcolm X is undoubtedly asking questions that can be termed "philosophical." As mentioned at the outset, the lack of written material by Malcolm X complicates the analysis if only because the history of the discipline of philosophy, since Socrates, has been based upon textual analysis. More carefully, the text under analysis in traditional philosophy is generally, with only rare exceptions, the individual effort of a thinker engaged in an effort to make an argument about a static problem. Malcolm X is involved in a dynamic engagement with an evolving societal problem as well as presenting his thinking to the public in the form of speeches, many of which have important ideas that are based upon current events or questions he has been asked by interlocutors about his understanding of these events.

This bears some analysis. In the present moment, the ability of what we can label public intellectuals, for the sake of argument, to present their ideas in real time is a twenty-first-century phenomenon totally dependent upon advances in communication technologies that invented "social media." We have to adjust our perception of events in the middle and late twentieth century to understand that thinker and interlocutor operate on a profoundly different temporal plane to the one we are

accustomed to. Further, the amount of curation that attends the production of traditional written discourse – books, essays, etc. – adds a
layer of filtering to that type of intellectual production as opposed to
conversation in real time. What I mean here is that Malcolm X's style of
knowledge production, considered undisciplined at the time, in many
ways presaged the nature of twenty-first-century communication in the
sense that it was uncurated, "on the fly," far closer in style to the forms of
"social media" discourse that we are accustomed to today.

It is important to consider that even beyond the style of communication in question, one must first acknowledge that what is fundamental
to this analysis is to understand that the primary difference between
Africana philosophy and the central lines of thought in the Western
philosophical tradition is the oppositional nature of the former, which is
primarily engaged in pushing against the imperatives of the latter.

Malcolm X, and most political philosophers of African descent
seemingly since Ptahhotep or the isolation of the Dogon people, are
developing political philosophy, theory and praxis against the context of
a dominant and coercive system of thinking that establishes its position
in a hierarchy of its own making by marginalizing people of African
descent. A thinker in this tradition is engaged in formulating modes of
understanding that speak to the reconstruction of Being from a position
of externally imposed sub-humanity. This thinking is exemplified by
the preoccupation of both Western and Africana philosophy with the
question of Being.

Western thinking on Being, taking Heidegger as one instantiation,
is preoccupied with understanding the nature of Being for the human
subject as existing at a distance, based upon the presence of reason as
the trait that establishes a separation from animals. The presupposition
in the Western philosophical tradition is that humans are necessarily
different from animals and the nature of this philosophical project is to
provide examples that offer assurance of this positive separation. What
is implicit in this thinking, particularly as it relates to the stratification of
humankind into human and sub-human, is the formation of the Negro
as exemplar of a subject existing as a lack or negative space with respect
to the essential elements of normative human-ness.

Malcolm X, along with other thinkers like him, is principally engaged
in a project of oppositional philosophy that is forced to address dominant
modes of thinking. With that understanding there are areas of focus that
seem to (pre)occupy the thinking of Malcolm X:

1. Recovering Black identity from externally imposed conditions of marginalization;
2. Establishing a sustainable identity within a political context that is designed to destabilize the Black subject;
3. Bridging the gap between civil and human rights in an effort to internationalize the struggle of Black people in America, and;
4. Developing a nationalist project that exists in opposition to and beyond traditionally constructed national boundaries.

It is important here to present what I believe to be, perhaps idiosyncratically on my part, Malcolm X's international relations theory, by which I mean that it may prove useful to reverse the vector of the common view of Malcolm X as a domestic activist who sees resonance with the problems that preoccupy him through analogy with struggles for independence outside of the United States, and instead to see his theory of the African–American subject as situating these figures as profoundly international actors in their radical exclusion from coherent citizenship in the realm of domestic politics. Stated differently, Malcolm understands the segregated environments and contexts of the lives of African–Americans not as analogously colonial but as a particular form of colonial existence that can only be properly understood and dismantled as a link in the chain of a complex series of international relationships that run uninterrupted back to the appearance of Columbus in the New World. The international relations corollary here would be the understanding of collective security as a form of robust diplomatic relations between sovereign nation-states that informs commonality and alliance, that for Malcolm X is best understood as a *collective insecurity* amongst similarly situated actors who suffer at the hands of structured hegemonic power. This thinking requires that we frame and understand the thinking of Malcolm X as it relates to the political thinking we label as Pan-Africanism both in theory and practice. What this means is that Malcolm X is interested in a relationship with the nations and people of Africa for the diasporic Africans in the "New World" that I intend to understand as deeply related to the logic and trajectory of his thought. However, it is important to note that Malcolm X's understanding of nationalism in this context, and here we must be thinking about the long discourse of something like Black nationalism, is necessarily improvisational around the classical understanding that nations require discernible geographic borders. Here, Lorde's assertion of the insufficiency of the master's tools for projects of radical political innovation is again relevant. In other words, there is a way in which considering a project of Black radical politics that grounds itself in the explicitly white supremacist notions of "Blood and Soil" in its must lurid representations is already to cede the ground of radicalism to a recursively doomed project of imitation of negative relations to political subjectivity. This will be considered more carefully in the exploration of the relationship of spatiality to Malcolm X's understanding of sovereignty and personal subjectivity in the chapters on the body and geographic space.

Before leaving the discussion of diaspora, there is an important linkage here to the thought of Edward Blyden elaborated in his booklet, "The Jewish Question", that should be referenced. The internationalist argument here is a permutation of the argument Blyden elaborates regarding the conceptualization of diaspora in a time and space well prior to the cataclysm of World War II and the ethnic cleansing of Jews by the Germans. Blyden's argument is ably handled in Michael J. C. Echeruo's essay, "Edward W. Blyden, 'The Jewish Question' and the Diaspora: Theory and Practice," published in 2010 in *The Journal of Black Studies*, in which he glosses Blyden's argument. Echeruo proposes first that Blyden understands that the question of Jewish diaspora provides an intellectual touchstone because his experience "... of being an African (American) who had also been tormented by the same kind of question."[24] The question that preoccupies what Blyden understands as the linkage between the two diasporas and what I understand to be the concern of Malcolm X is articulated in an extract from the article. Echeruo writes:

Accordingly, although the nationalities seeking recognition within Europe shared a common (Christian) religious culture, the Jewish population of Europe, scattered as it was in these various nationalities-in-formation, presented a rather special case, not having the cohesive fact of territory to define its nationhood but having a long and distinguished history of state-hood which was, however, bound up with the very basis of their identity, namely, Judaism as an inalienable heritage. Hence, although, on one hand, they were severely persecuted in many parts of Europe and, on the other, were strongly integrated into society in others, they could have no parallel claim, as other nationalities apparently could, to a "land" of their own. And because, for all Jews, so the reasoning went in these discussions, identity was inseparable from origins – that is, from a chosen-ness bound up, as it were, in the fact of a god-given land and an eternal covenant of God with the people *as a people*, a frequently paralyzing paradox was inescapable. They were, in a phrase Du Bois would use of the African American several decades later, echoing Martin Delany, a nation within a nation.[25]

This important concept of "a nation within a nation" and the imperative of an awareness of the terms and conditions of diaspora, serves as the preoccupation of Malcolm X's thought process that I will endeavor to tease apart to facilitate its careful examination.

With that understanding, this project will attempt to unfold the political philosophy of Malcolm X by separating it into four areas: (1) ontology, (2) the body, (3) geographic space and (4) revolution. Some notes on the decision to proceed in this manner may be helpful to some. As a practical matter, the sheer amount of material produced by Malcolm X in his public role is overwhelming: one temptation is to embark on a type of historically-based analysis that begins sometime after his release from prison and ends with his final moments at the podium in the Audubon Ballroom. This doesn't fit with the effort here to attempt to assemble an understanding of the overarching intellectual framework in which Malcolm X developed what I am proposing is a coherent philosophical system.

I have developed a path through this ideological thicket that begins with ontology. This is somewhat obvious, in that beginnings are just that, but here the focus will be the project of assembling an ontological subjectivity for the diasporic Black body that recognizes the existence of the enslaved condition but endeavors to construct a bridge over it back to the moments before that catastrophe, without losing track of the devastating context. The next step in the path will be an attempt to expose the embodied nature of this philosophical system.

In this introduction I have mentioned the corporeal nature of Malcolm X's thought and will demonstrate how the body becomes the manner in which he lends coherence and the mechanism for the praxis of the imperative of his ontological project of reclamation of the self-referential and externally recognized sovereignty of the self. The next step in the thinking of Malcolm X is understanding how this body resolves and stabilizes its existence.

This will be examined in the chapter entitled "Geographic Space," which will mark how the thinking of Malcolm X endeavors to resolve the transnational nature of the diasporic corpus by destabilizing the borders of the body and the space it inhabits. The final chapter arrives at the *telos* of this thinking, the question of revolution.

In many ways, the multilayered deconstruction and reconstruction of political and personal subjectivity can only be resolved by the alteration of the atmospheric political, economic and social conditions that serve to authorize the creation and continued existence of the subaltern. As with most things, the popular understanding of revolution in the thinking of Malcolm X as being a project of violence is reductive and the complexity of what he understands as the bloodless revolution will be examined in detail.

1

Ontology

The question of ontology in the thinking of Malcolm X is complicated in several ways, not least of which being the fact that the ontological condition of the "so-called Negro" is encumbered from a perspective of resolving the inclusion of this figure in the category of "human." With that in mind, what presages this question is the necessity of asserting that the thinking of the figure so named and established as the Negro has the capacity (a) to be considered as human and (b) possesses rationality sufficient to allow for individual sovereignty that facilitates full participation in a societal order. What I am proposing here is an echo of an idea presented in the Introduction that proposes that the thinking of Malcolm X on ontology exists in an intellectual genealogy that is bounded (roughly) by the thinking of W. E. B. Du Bois and Frantz Fanon as it relates to establishing the identity of the "Negro" and provides the tactics for dismantling that condition.

In approaching the philosophical thought of Malcolm X there is an obvious path that begins with his involvement with the Nation of Islam during his period of incarceration. What we have gleaned from the biographical presentation of this period is that the Nation of Islam provided a systematized educational program and religion for Malcolm Little after a period of his life that can generously be characterized as "wayward." I believe this to be true, but this effort would be remiss if it did not take up the counter-culture in which the young Malcolm found himself – that is, arguably, a particular way of being for people who are separated from the benefits of full citizenship that underscores an argument for distinct "phases" of his intellectual development. Malcolm X, as a thinker, traversed three distinct periods that are all based upon a critical engagement with the dominant/normative political philosophical order. The first was a period of existence that I will call "static counter-cultural existence/being" which was marked by his persistent involvement in a sub-economy that, at its most extreme, relied upon criminality. The "static" nature mentioned here is meant to expose just that: this is a potentially moribund state of existence. This stage of existence was not predicated on altering that conditionality. The second begins with his enlightenment and education by the Nation of Islam while incarcerated for his activities in phase one and ends roughly with his silencing by Elijah Muhammad. The final phase is probably accurately described as his working through categories of thought that we now understand as post-colonial. This is bounded by his journey to Mecca and locations in Africa and his assassination. Malcolm X is struggling, in each of these stages of his intellectual development, to formulate a philosophy and theory of subaltern political existence within the dominant and oppressive political context. There are several elements of his thought that are consistent across these distinct periods. He develops theoretical positions for (1) living within the dominant political system, (2) methods for disrupting that system, and (3) imagining a future both within the coercive system (that is, the system of stasis in phase one) and a future in a "new" revolutionary political reality in phases two and three.

The argument that I am presenting amounts to stating that the hegemonic nature of American political culture that serves to marginalize the political, social and economic lives of the "Other," in this case, African–Americans, establishes the conditions for a counter-culture to exist as the inevitable way of being. By establishing the "so-called Negro" as always outside of coherent and robust participation in governance, this subject is left few choices. This establishes a specific type of marginalized subjectivity that disallows banal political existence. There is a broad statement regarding the nature of political philosophy that I wish to underscore.

Efforts on the part of arguably "universalist" arguments regarding the provenance of philosophical thought often turn on a reading practice similar to that employed in literature that requires the "disappearance of the author" from the analysis. What this means generally is that serious philosophical thinking is purported to have been conducted at some distance from the biographical facts of the philosopher who has produced the philosophical system. What this allows is a type of abstraction of political context that, in theory, facilitates the transportation of systems of thought beyond the context of their existence. An example of this is the Western preoccupation with systems of thinking from the fifth century B.C. The idea that Aristotle, for one example, was a thinker of sufficient power that he was able to distance himself from the context of his existence and produce ideas that are sufficiently abstract to represent something like "timeless truth," exemplifies this notion.

At the beginning of this book I mentioned the difficulty of disentangling the activist Malcolm X from the political philosopher Malcolm X. The problem is perhaps more complex in that it speaks to this Western preoccupation with philosophical thought that privileges the notion of abstract rationality that allows distance from life circumstance. The notion that people of African descent demonstrate a lack of reason through an inability to exercise this form of personal exorcism of the self from the condition of the self in order to facilitate universal thinking negatively prefigures the conversation regarding the thinking of Malcolm X in this realm. Neither of these conditions is supported by facts: "philosophers" recognized by the Western canon are *not* divorced from their personal circumstances and people of African descent who speak to a specific social context are *not* revealing an inability to demonstrate elevated thinking by doing so. It is only necessary here to background the biographical Malcolm X because his thinking can find the marginalia of biography overwhelming the text that is to be the preoccupation of the project. This requires the effort here to walk a fine line that I believe actually demonstrates the complexity of the project facing a thinker like Malcolm X.

What I am proposing is that one result of subjective marginalization, understood here as the creation of political subjects whose political existence is in fact meant to demonstrate the imperative to disallow their political viability because (in large manner) their grip on rationality renders them ineligible for positive political existence, makes it impossible for these same subjects to think philosophically about ameliorating their condition. This means that a thinker like Malcolm X has to operate in an environment that simultaneously recognizes and disavows subjective marginalization. The subject situated in this position, in order to imagine (from a perspective that allows thinking in the realm of political philosophy) must (1) simultaneously be aware of the forces of marginalization that assail them; (2) understand that this condition represents the prevailing context of their political existence; (3) understand that "thinking" cannot be divorced completely from its prevailing social context; (4) through this understanding be able to redeploy the forces of marginalization to create intellectual force to deconstruct that circumstance, and (5) be prepared to maintain subjective existence through the process of subjective deconstruction otherwise known as remaining sane.

This may appear abstract, but an examination of the question regarding the evolution of Malcolm X's thinking on a return to Africa for diasporic people of African descent demonstrates the practical application of this thought experiment. Further, this is where we can witness the intellectual structure that upholds the project of something like "Black nationalism" that we will find is able to use the geographic and legalistic structures that are implicated in anti-Black racism to serve as the locus of political viability. As mentioned in the Introduction, there are four themes that outline the thinking examined here. These four points outline the path I will follow to trace the essential elements of Malcolm X's thinking that are preoccupied with three manifestations of social injustice: political, social and economic. They are:

1. Recovering Black identity;
2. Establishing sustainable subjectivity;
3. Bridging the gap between civil and human rights; and
4. Developing a national project.

That being understood, the foundation of Malcolm X's thinking is based upon a process of restoring what he understands to be positive subjective self-regard and recognition. When I say the "foundation," what I am proposing here is that there is a particular epistemological element to this thinking that is based upon a system of morality that antecedes what I have described as the more obvious involvement of Malcolm X with the theological and ethical systems of the Nation of Islam. This epistemological formation is related to the always/already oppositional existence of the Black subject in the coercive context of white supremacy. These structures oppose positive identity formation that then renders it a project of radical reformation of the subject to achieve robust political, social and economic existence.

Stated simply, Malcolm X, prior to "becoming" Malcolm X through the praxis of a syncretic version of Islam, was intellectually invested in a form of morality that holds governmental structures accountable for the destruction of positive subjectivity. This accountability for regimes of power designed to do harm appears in the thinking of Malcolm X in two important ways. First, he argues that the first role (or goal) of the oppressor is to persuade the subject under assault to doubt the efficacy of their relationship and status in a given political perception. This leads to the second stage of this project, which renders political oppression inevitable in a dual vector: the oppressor oppresses because the subject under assault is ineligible for positive political identity and the oppressed, led to believe that they are "worthless," are not in a position to develop projects of political viability, much less revolution, because there is no legitimacy as understood by the community of actors who are believed to validate the viability of political projects. This is not "new" thinking and identifying its relationship to the thinking of W. E. B. Du Bois and Frantz Fanon on this subject lends depth to the argument that Malcolm X provides an important intellectual bridge between these two canonical thinkers. This requires careful consideration.

Broadly understood, W. E. B. Du Bois, in his *The Souls of Black Folk*, establishes the existence of two related concepts that define the political existence of Black people in America: the "color line" and his formulation of Second-Sight, Double Consciousness and Two-ness, which I call "tripartite subaltern self-consciousness." In *The Souls of Black Folk*, Du Bois proposes, ultimately, a putatively unsolvable binary relationship between the Negro and the American. Recall the canonical passage that is relevant here:

> After the Egyptian and Indian, the Greek and Roman, the Teuton and Mongolian, the Negro is a sort of seventh son, born with a veil, and gifted with second-sight in this American world – a world which yields him no true self-consciousness, but ONLY lets him see himself through the revelation of the other world. It is a peculiar sensation, this double-consciousness, this sense of ALWAYS looking at one's self through the eyes of others, of measuring one's soul by the tape of a world that looks on in amused contempt and pity. One EVER feels his two-ness – an American, a Negro; two souls, two thoughts, two unreconciled strivings; two warring ideals in one dark body, whose dogged strength alone keeps it from being torn asunder.[1]

There is a penchant in Africana scholarship generally and scholarship surrounding Du Bois specifically, to focus on Double Consciousness. The reason I emphasize the tripartite nature of his formulation – Second-Sight, Double Consciousness, and Two-ness – is to mark the cause and effect relationship, beginning with Second-Sight, passing through Double Consciousness and ending with Two-ness as representative of a complex way of being that includes, in its manifold relationship of these discretely complex ideas, a way to dismantle its logic. In giving careful and close consideration to this foundational system of thought, it is necessary to indulge in an exercise in hermeneutics to tease out a way forward through this complex idea. Here it is useful to revisit the elements of this passage from Du Bois one at a time:

> After the Egyptian and Indian, the Greek and Roman, the Teuton and Mongolian, the Negro is a sort of seventh son, born with a veil, and gifted with second-sight in this American world – a world which yields him no true self-consciousness, but ONLY lets him see himself through the revelation of the other world.[2]

This passage requires close and careful attention, particularly in light of the fact that we find an important turn of phrase that delineates three things: the "world"; a particular way of seeing it; and the effect of the first two. First, the Negro, in this account, is "gifted" with this way of seeing in "this American world," leaving open the question of whether, in Du Bois' formulation at the time, Second-Sight might be present in other worlds or in other subjects. Second, it is the "world which yields him no true self-consciousness." This concept has to be held close to the forefront of any thinking engaged in unravelling this proposal. The implication is that Second-Sight is a way of seeing that exists independently of awareness of the fact of its existence. Stated differently, Du Bois is proposing that America, as it exists, does not provide for the existence of true self-consciousness for the Negro. This is different than a false notion of self-consciousness existing because of a way of perceiving the self. For instance, it doesn't matter whether you believe in or are aware of gravity as such or not. It acts independently of cognition. Finally, the last phrase, "… but ONLY lets him see himself through the revelation of the other world," requires that we deal with the cause and effect relationship between revelation of the other world and only seeing himself through it.

With respect to the framing here as "revelation," I read the passage as relating to this understanding as a product of the veil, as Du Bois positions it in his account, the divide between Black and white; his "color-line." In other words, it is a structural fact of this Manichean world that the Negro has no true self-consciousness.

At this stage we are left to decide whether Second-Sight is seeing oneself through the revelation of another or is in fact a way of being aware that you are seeing yourself through the eyes of another, which I take as two very different propositions. Second-Sight will be situated as the cognition of the fact of a lack of true self-consciousness as opposed to a way of seeing that is itself the cause of this problem. I am proposing that this passage implicates Second-Sight as a form of consciousness that allows the Negro awareness of the fact of a lack of true self-consciousness as a result of a separation between Black and white.

It seems clear from the text that Du Bois structures a clear "if–then" statement. If there is Second-Sight, then there is Double Consciousness and further Two-ness. Moving forward in Du Bois' text from where we left off we can examine his proposition.

It is a peculiar sensation, this double-consciousness, this sense of always looking at one's self through the eyes of others, of measuring one's soul by the tape of a world that looks on in amused contempt and pity.[3]

Du Bois describes Double Consciousness as a "peculiar sensation," not a mode of cognition as such. Second-Sight remains the manner of perception and Double Consciousness the sensation that observation causes. Du Bois, in this account, positions the Negro as profoundly sensitive to the stimulation of Second-Sight. Therefore it seems clear that Double Consciousness can neither exist without nor antecede Second-Sight. This leaves us with Two-ness to address. Returning to the text:

One ever feels his two-ness – an American, a Negro; two souls, two thoughts, two unreconciled strivings; two warring ideals in one dark body, whose dogged strength alone keeps it from being torn asunder.[4]

Two-ness is understood here as a feeling that I wish to consider in relation to the notion of "sensation." The way I would like to parse the difference is to propose that a "feeling," in this context, requires a type of cultural awareness or perhaps a premonitionary stance in that sensations can be felt independently of context, cultural or otherwise. It seems here that Du Bois is using feeling in the sense of it being linked to an understanding of what the sensation of Double Consciousness causes the subject to feel: the separation of mind and body ("I think therefore I am").

All of that being said, and further recognizing the existence of an instance of mechanical causality that I am proposing exists here that is resistant to separation of the parts from the whole of this thinking, it is Two-ness that serves as the path forward to Fanon through Malcolm X. Du Bois, for his part, gives us a set of physical and metaphysical relations that have to be accounted for prior to interrogating the assemblage also known as "civil society" that may or may not include certain subjects and in fact may only be considered whole through a process of selective dys-inclusion. What Du Bois accomplishes here is to situate the "Black body" as different from the Negro and its opposite, in this formulation, the American. This thinking requires us to enter into a practice of translation between Du Bois' "Negro" and our "Black" in order to hold onto the argument presented here and not allow the disappearance of the Negro from our language to fool us into believing that the phenomenon of the Negro has been eradicated or rendered anachronistic.

At the other end of the poles of thinking that I am proposing here exists the thought of Frantz Fanon. The reference in this case is his critical examination of Black subjectivity in *Black Skin, White Masks*. In this text, Fanon is preoccupied with the depravity of intra-subjective awareness of Black subjects for themselves; a state of affairs that can broadly be labeled as self-hatred and is another way of articulating what Du Bois considers a lack of "true self-consciousness." In Fanon's text, the author unpacks what he understands as the context that confronts Black subjects who are marginalized through a number of harmful assumptions.

What may be useful here is to imagine the Black body as a space of political construction. Further, if we understand that political space, and the establishment and maintenance of a border, as a practice of coercion, the language of revolutionary change that populates Fanon's narrative regarding the recovery of Black identity can (must?) be read as analogous to the radical deconstruction and reconstruction of political space. This border can be either one of the subject's own creation that serves to secure something like "privacy" or one imposed upon the subject that functions something like a prison wall. This presents a dilemma of an existential nature. If the subject (dis)forming content of a political space is identified and evacuated and that space is "refilled" with an alternative way of Being that does not alter the coercive geographic boundaries of the state, what are the prospects for radical change or stable existence? If the internal political "stuff" is altered inside a self-imposed boundary, is the thing really the same? Alternatively, if the subject alters the status of the self inside an externally-imposed carceral state of being, what really changes? Further, if we understand that the Black body exists as a politically constructed space of absolute "Othering," as it evacuates itself one might necessarily be concerned with what becomes of the evacuated frame while it awaits alteration in a world system that remains committed to a continuation of a state of Black subaltern existence? Fanon establishes the fractured ontological ground from which he intends to fight through the Hegelian dialectic:

> At the risk of encouraging the resentment of my brothers of color, I will say that the black is not a man.
>
> There is a zone of non-being, an extraordinarily sterile and arid region, a bare ramp from which a new emergence can arise. In the majority of cases, the Black is not able to benefit from this descent into a veritable Hell.[5]

As I mentioned previously, the project from the perspective of Du Bois is to locate the prospect for identity recreation as the cause of the effect of political viability through awareness of the fact of marginalization (Second-Sight) that leads ultimately to consciousness of the incompatibility of Blackness and American-ness (Two-ness). Du Bois, in *Souls*, "solves" this problematic through a project of education of talented members of Black society that becomes the mechanism for recognition of political and social viability on the part of the structures of power that established and maintained this marginalization. Fanon approaches this, at least in *Black Skin, White Masks*, through a series of critical self-reflections that *strip* the subject in question down so that they are able to enter what he refers to as "the zone of non-being," which is a space for the recreation of identity. Two things are important here. Ultimately, Fanon lands on revolutionary violence as the method to resolve this problem in the same way that Du Bois proposes education as the most effective solution.

Malcolm X, in his most evolved thinking represents a combination of both of these systems of revolutionary subject re-making. It is important to note that both Du Bois and Fanon propose radically secular methods for creating sovereign subjects. By addressing the ontological foundation of the thinking of Malcolm X, we witness the outline of what I have labeled as his brand of "Black political theology."

In addressing the political subject that is disallowed a positive position in this societal order and subsequently a persistent negative understanding of the self, Malcolm X, throughout his career, is invested in naming self-hatred as an exemplar of this phenomenon, while at the same time seeking to identify methodologies for breaking its grip on the subject. As a practical matter, the intra-subjective awakening that happened for Malcolm Little while in prison establishes the ontological foundation of a project of radical self-recreation in the face of coercive threat that is aimed at the establishment of a positive political and economic project.

The Nation of Islam proposes that an essential step along the path of reclamation of identity and a recalibration with the divine status of Black people was to fracture the naming practices of Western societal order, particularly as it relates to the patriarchal system of chattel slavery. The argument is fairly straightforward: Black people in America have lost their identity and that continued condition of shattered subjectivity is perpetuated by the loss of a coherent relationship to African genealogy. This might reductively be perceived as an idiosyncratic attempt by members of the Nation of Islam to create a false identity that has no political viability. However, the vehemence of the attacks launched by critics of the Nation of Islam generally, and at Malcolm X specifically, forced him to acknowledge that his "real" name implied that there is something that practitioners of white supremacy recognize as important enough to destroy.

There are several instances of this phenomenon, but here I will focus on an interview on the Chicago based program "City Desk" on March 17, 1963. The free-ranging interview is generally focused on comments Malcolm X made regarding a plane crash that claimed the lives of tourists from Georgia who were visiting France, but as part of the introduction of the panelist, the moderator is careful to introduce Malcolm X as a representative of the Nation of Islam who "calls himself Malcolm X." This is in contradistinction to the manner in which all the other members of the panel are introduced, all of whom are referenced by their names, without the qualifier that implies that Malcolm is presenting an alias. A careful examination of this important interview exemplifies the intellectually violent context in which Malcolm X functions as a political thinker and philosopher.

The moderator of "City Desk," Jim Hurlbut, after establishing the "outside" nature of their guest, Malcolm X, asks a series of questions regarding the "platform" of the Nation of Islam. Malcolm X makes a broad claim, attributed to the "Honorable Elijah Muhammad" that the NoI stands for a form of radical personal and collective freedom for Black people in the United States. Hurlbut wonders if this is a form of abstract hatred of the white race that, in spite of Malcolm X's claims that that is not a part of NoI doctrine, could be adopted by acolytes of the faith who misinterpret what is meant by the freedom of Black people. It seems clear that Hurlbut finds Black freedom to be authorized and maintained by a hatred of white people that, one might surmise, would only matter to him because it might lead to the political, social and economic subjugation of white people by the "Other". The relationship between Black freedom and the destruction of white people implied by Hurlbut is quickly dismissed by Malcolm X, who then establishes the framework for his own thinking by proclaiming the relationship of the term "Negro" to slavery and thereby allowing no departure from the necessity of Black political viability in the twentieth century to a linkage to its absolute lack under the coercive regime of chattel slavery. The path that Hurlbut wishes to establish is that the doctrine of the NoI is at best inadvertently based upon abstract hatred of white people, while Malcolm X insists on establishing at least two important discursive points that are specific to this discussion and speak to the broader claim made here that something like Africana political philosophy is *always* oppositional.

The first point has been established earlier in this text: that white supremacy has created an environment that establishes and maintains the political, social and economic marginalization of Black people. The second point is that opposition to that fact is not based upon abstract dislike of the perpetrators of that condition but particular opposition to the presence of what Malcolm X labels here as "evil." The larger point, manifest by the moderator's insistence that Black viability is equivalent to hatred of white people (this is the fruit of the poisonous tree of the opposition to the claim "Black Lives Matter" by insisting that "All Lives Matter" or worse "Blue Lives Matter") is the core of the need by white interlocutors abstractly to resist the coherence of the arguments presented by Malcolm X.

The discussion between Malcolm X and Hurlbut shifts to the question of naming, and its relationship to the regime of chattel slavery in the mind of Malcolm X. When Malcolm X employs the phrase "the 'so-called' Negro," Hurlbut seizes on it and asks him to elaborate. The text of his response is instructive and illustrates the logic Malcolm X wishes to establish between people of African descent being called "Negroes" and what Du Bois calls a lack of "true self-consciousness."

Malcolm X: Mr Muhammad teaches us that Negro is a term applied during slavery by the slave master. And right today it is a term used to point out the descendants of slaves. It is never used for black people period. Africans can come to this country and they aren't called Negroes and if they are called Negroes they resent it. So if Negro meant Black as we have been taught it would be a term that could be applicable or appliable to everyone but he says that it is something that meant slave or something that has been left out of society politically, economically, educationally, and otherwise.

Hurlbut: You don't think of it as an anthropological term?

Malcolm X: Definitely it is not an anthropological term. It is a slave term. And it was a term that was invented in America and was used by the slave makers, slave traders, and slave masters and attached to the property or chattel or merchandise that our people represented in that particular day.[6]

This exchange requires close and careful analysis. As mentioned above, this is an important discursive shift on the part of Malcolm X that is meant to establish and deny genealogy at the same time. Malcolm X is establishing a genealogy of oppression that is "denied" by interlocutors like Hurlbut who view notions of Black political viability as necessarily hostile to white people. This establishes at least an explicit notion of several things in the minds of white supremacists like Hurlburt: (1) the marginalization of Black people by structures of white power are *not* related to forms of hatred; (2) the rejection of that condition by Black people is tantamount to hatred of white people, and (3) to be Black and politically viable is to undermine the existence of white people. Malcolm X rejects all three of these notions and requires that Hurlbut (as representative of this mode of thinking on the part of white supremacists) recognizes the culpability of white people in this condition and accepts that if there is hatred introduced into the system, that is the fault of white people. This is part and parcel of the theological argument being advanced by Malcolm X and the Nation of Islam that the misfortunes of white people (as indicated by the plane crash that serves as an important element of this interview) are the necessary result of their own evil. The world would see this again with Malcolm X's notorious "chickens have come home to roost" statement, regarding the assassination of President Kennedy.

Malcolm X's understanding that the term "Negro" as applied to the bodies of Black people is in fact a misrepresentation of the facts is encompassed in his insistence of employing "so-called" as the modifier of the term. This is interesting, in that it is inseparable from the employment by Hurlbut of the notion that Malcolm X "calls himself" by the name he has chosen, explicitly requiring that he is the "so-called" Malcolm X just as Malcolm X understands himself as a "so-called" Negro. This is the metaphysical ground that Malcolm X identifies as the intellectual foundation of physical oppression, and its denial on the part of interlocutors is to obscure the fact of its existence while at the same time establishing its power. This panel understands this discourse regarding naming as important. The reasons for that importance are never made explicit but I will propose an understanding of "why" that I believe is supported by the text here and is inextricably related to my earlier claim that the notion that the "X" represents a foolish attempt at creating a mythology is belied by the all-out assault against its employment. It appears that the imperative to destabilize this practice might relate itself to a perception by white supremacists that it begins to undermine the coherence of the Western political project and its relationship to the ("so-called") Negro.

Returning to the text of the interview, we find that Malcolm X clearly understands or recognizes the viability of the teachings of the Nation of Islam that the status of the Negro is in fact a current manifestation of the condition of slavery. His final point on the lack of the relation of the term Negro to "anthropology," in the way that Hurlbut wishes to use it, unleashes a way of thinking that understands naming in this sense as a particular form of coercive violence that constitutes, transports and maintains marginalized political subjectivity. This is reified by the disaggregation of "slavery" generally into component parts of making, moving and maintaining. This is productively understood as an articulation from the perspective of Malcolm X as a political philosopher as not dissimilar to the claims advanced by Walter Benjamin in his important essay "Critique of Violence" that proposes that there are various forms of political violence that either constitute or are constituting of political subjects or more carefully, law-establishing and law-maintaining violence. What Malcolm X seems to be contextualizing here is a careful delineation of the stages of the enslaved condition, with the slave-maker establishing the ontology of radical modes of un-freedom, the slave-trader invested in the transportation of that status from potential to kinetic activity, and finally the slave-master who maintains and exploits that conditionality. What he seems to be emphasizing here is that the conditionality of slavery is maintained in his contemporary context with the label Negro, which we find is the state of being for Black people that is further manifested by the cultural erasure and linguistic possession of Black bodies displayed in the employment of Western surnames.

The moderator passes the conversation on to another panel member, Len O'Connor, who immediately takes up the question of naming by unceremoniously demanding that Malcolm X reveal on the broadcast "his real name." This exchange is fascinating, in that the questioner seems to agree with the genealogy that Malcolm X is proposing, demanding to know his "Father's last name" and ultimately to demand an answer to whether:

> Was there any line; any point in the genealogy of your family when you did have to use the last name and if so what was it?[7]

There are important points that can be gleaned from a close reading of this encounter: one relates to a broader argument regarding the philosophical methodology of Malcolm X and the other is specific to this question of naming and its relationship to oppression as well as the possibility of overcoming that condition. I will take up the former question first, in that it will establish an important point of reference for an understanding of what is going on here in the thought of Malcolm X methodologically.

Some background is important. In preparing for this project I spent a great deal of time talking through the ins and outs of a productive approach to the complexity of dealing with the discursive nature of Malcolm X's thought. One important conversation was with Raphael Sassower, a Professor of Philosophy at the University of Colorado at Colorado Springs. What Professor Sassower proposed is that there is a way in which the dialogic nature of Malcolm X's philosophical approach is productively understood as "Socratic." That is true in an important sense, but there is a layer of complexity here that essentially inverts the structure of that classical framework. This is underscored in this interaction. O'Connor attempts to employ Socratic questioning to intellectually "guide" Malcolm X to the conclusion that (a) "X" is not his name, (b) he has a legal name, and (c) that legal name is related to patriarchal genealogy in the Western tradition, all of which implodes the philosophical intervention being proposed here, in a way that is very different to the way in which Socrates uses questioning to reify his philosophical point.

As mentioned above, Malcolm X does not resist, necessarily, the veracity of points (b) and (c) above, but understands them to be a manifestation of oppression: his resistance both marks and undermines that condition. What I propose here is that the Socratic method is inverted, in that Malcolm X is framed as subordinate to the questioner and it is that attempted subordination that requires his resistance to the status of his identity proposed by his interlocutor. His resistance exposes the form of that subordination while inverting it through this dialogic resistance that undermines the point of the questioner and establishes his philosophical position from a place of opposition and struggle. This illustrates the point made in the Introduction to this book that proposed that Africana thought, by its nature, is oppositional and in that point of departure necessarily differs from the Western philosophical tradition.

Moving to the substance of this discussion, it is interesting to pursue the question of genealogy that both Malcolm X and O'Connor center in this exchange. It is obvious that Malcolm X is establishing the genealogical/ontological relationship of slavery to the "so-called" Negro and the mark of possession that is manifest by the employment of naming practices from the enslaved condition. O'Connor insists upon that naming practice as related to genealogy but has erected an intellectual firewall around the implications of slavery as the causal condition of that naming practice. O'Connor's question to Malcolm X regarding whether he had gone to court to establish "X" as his legal name lends credence to the claim made here that this is productively read through Benjamin's notion of law-establishing and law-maintaining violence. Here, the proposal that accepted legal structures are to be employed in order to recognize a project of resistance to structures of law-establishing violence is the crux of the matter. Malcolm X here marks out an exclusion from the employment of the structures of power as useful in projects of radical politics at the point of naming or, more carefully, resistance to naming through a process of *renaming*, as illustrative of a process of reclamation of self-sovereignty or "true" self-consciousness.

The final move here, ultimately when Malcolm X distances himself further from Western naming convention and its depraved relationship to the marginalization of the Black subject and the Nation of Islam by becoming El-Hajj Malik el-Shabazz. This event is ably handled by

Saladin Ambar in his essential text, *Malcolm X at Oxford Union: Racial Politics in a Global Era*, where he writes:

> For Malcolm, his transformation represented a kind of double freedom – becoming X was a freedom from white identity and familial ties. Becoming *El-Hajj Malik El-Shabazz* was a freedom from organizational orthodoxy within the NOI and its deviation from acceptable Islamic teachings. And yet, by remaining X and Malik El-Shabazz, Malcolm was holding onto two visions of himself and his politics. He was linking himself to the black diaspora in the "Western Hemisphere", as he responded to Berkeley at Oxford; and he was forging ties to the broader *Dar al-Islam* – the Muslim world that he had already joined to great personal satisfaction.[8]

The philosophical question that reveals itself here is simply stated as: Why is this so important?

The question that presaged this section: "Why is the white establishment so preoccupied with this practice of (re)naming?" cuts both ways. What I mean is what is the matter here both for Malcolm X, who has drawn a distinction that establishes the importance of naming, and the fact that this process has attracted the attention and palpable ire ("What is your real name?") from those who resist this project. I mentioned in the Introduction that there is a way in which this practice of replacing the surnames of its members with an "X" by the Nation of Islam can be viewed as symbolic in a way that is devoid of larger political implication in the same way that the name my parents chose for me is largely without context beyond my bounded personhood. Additionally, as a practical matter, parents are virtually unfettered in naming their child whatever they please and an adult is equally free to change their name to whatever they please, whenever they see fit. If it were true that all adults were free to change their names, then it would not produce the vitriolic response of interlocutors like O'Connor, who in this interview goes on to label the NoI as a "cult."[9]

This naming process needs to be considered from two perspectives: theological and philosophical. Further, I argue that the combination of these modes of thought allows us to establish the intellectual providence of what I have called Black political theology and the way it manifests itself in the thinking of Malcolm X as he operates through and with the foundational arguments of Elijah Muhammad's syncretic practice of Islam. The philosophical aspect of this theological practice is, in my reading, a manifestation of the combination of what I have called Du Bois' "Tripartite Subaltern Self-Consciousness" and Fanon's "zone of non-being."

It is imperative to interrogate the practice of naming in the Western theological tradition as the context from which the resistance or alteration of naming manifests substantive resistance to the divine imprimatur of governance. The link between practices of oppression, control and naming is the first step in unpacking this thinking. To develop this idea, the opening moments of *Genesis* are instructive. Adam, upon his animation by God, is given the task of naming the animals in the Garden of Eden. After creating Adam, placing him in the Garden and noting the presence of the problematic Tree(s), the question of naming presents itself. As a practical matter, Verse 8 of Chapter 2 of *Genesis* names the Garden as Eden, so it is to be assumed that the text is sympathetic to understanding that as the "true" name of the Garden, in that it is coterminous with the Will of God and His creation. Additionally, it is clear from the text that the notion of the first human being known as "Adam" is in actuality what he "is," not what he is named, recalling the notes on this passage presented by Robert Alter in his essential text, *The First Five Books of Moses: A Translation with Commentary*. It seems, therefore, that God reserves for himself the naming of certain types of creation as the text illustrates, picking up at the start of Verse 10.

> Now a river runs out of Eden to water the garden and from there splits off into four streams. The name of the first is Pishon ... [a]nd the name of the second river is Gihon ... And the name of the third river is Tigris ... [a]nd the fourth is Euphrates.[10]

The text here seems to situate God as the naming agent of the "non-living" features of the world and the plants, but Adam is granted the power of naming the "living creatures" in the absence of explaining where the names of these rivers originate, if not with the unmediated Will of God.

> And the Lord God fashioned from the soil each beast of the field and each fowl of the heavens and brought each to the human to see what he would call it, and whatever the human called a living creature, that was its name. And the human called names to all the cattle and to the

fowl of the heavens, and to all the beasts of the field, but for the human no sustainer beside him was found. (*Genesis 2: 19–21*)

This theological construct, "Adamic Naming," giving both name and function to an entity, is what is at stake here in the Nation of Islam's understanding of the relationship between the names of Black people and the notion of possession that is the foundation of the enslaved condition. What the NoI argue, and Malcolm X promotes in the discourse examined here, is that the notion of mastery over the bodies of Black people granted the slave-holder the same divine imprimatur granted Adam: ". . . and whatever the human called a living creature, that was its name." The argument is fairly straightforward. The ability to "rename" enslaved humans, erasing their name and culture, during the process of slave-making, allowed the coercive power to express itself in the total alteration of subjective identity while at the same time giving these beings their function. This "function" exists orders of magnitude beyond the simple notion of defining employment but includes the total-izing of the lack of even the possibility of subjective freedom through self-identification, what Du Bois would call "true self-consciousness." What the NoI proposes, as expressed by the argument presented under the pressure of these hostile interlocutors by Malcolm X, is that the legacy of this subjective destruction through *Adamic Naming* on the part of the master class continues in the contemporary moment in the manifest subjugation of Black people labeled as "Negroes" and as the possession of slave-masters through the continued use of Western slave names. This is where the corrective destruction of the subject proposed by Fanon is apparent in the thinking of Malcolm X and the NoI. Further, we find the concept of naming and freedom masterfully explored in the diasporic African literary tradition most canonically in the work of Toni Morrison, who takes up this problem in *Song of Solomon*.

In that novel, Morrison destabilizes the biblical concept of Adamic Naming in order to render it useful in understanding the lives of mar-ginalized Black people. In the novel, the patriarch of the Dead family, Macon Dead, reflects on the unique naming practice of his family. Morrison writes:

Surely, he thought. He and his sister had some ancestor, some lithe young man with onyx skin and legs as straight as cane stalks, who had a name that was real. A name given to him at birth with love and seriousness. A name that was not a joke, nor a disguise, nor a brand name. But who this lithe young man was, and where his cane-stalk legs carried him from or to, could never be known. No. Nor his name. His own parents, in some mood of perverseness or resignation, had agreed to abide by a naming done to them by somebody who couldn't have cared less. Agreed to pass on to all their issue this heavy name scrawled in perfect thoughtlessness by a drunken Yankee in the Union Army. A literal slip of the pen handed to his father on a piece of paper and which he handed on to his only son, and his son likewise handed to his; Macon Dead who begat a second Macon Dead who married Ruth Foster (Dead) and begat Magdalene called Lena Dead and First Corinthians Dead and (when he least expected it) another Macon Dead, now known to the better part of the world as Milkman Dead. And as if that were not enough, a sister named Pilate Dead …

He had cooperated as a young father with the blind selection of names from the Bible for every child other than the first male. And abided by whatever the finger pointed to, for he knew every configuration of the naming of his sister.[11]

For Morrison, the seemingly random practice of choosing names by blindly pointing to a page in the Bible is implicated with the genealogy of the enslaved condition and patriarchy. At the moment of emancipation by the Union soldiers it is a thoughtless relationship to the personhood of the subject that creates the recurring naming practice of the first male born. Further, the notion of the random selection of names from the lexicon of the language is restricted by the requirement that the name can only be drawn from the interior of the Christian Bible. The NoI endeavors to elide the first and third of these conditions while leaving the second, patriarchy, in place and uninterrogated. The challenge for this attempt to eliminate the straight-line relationship to the enslaved condition also has to deal with the restrictive nature of language.

The argument I am presenting here is that the replacement of "slave names" with the mathematical variable "X" represents the practical manifestation of Fanon's "zone of non-being": a position of positive subjective erasure that provides a point of departure for the recreation of the subject from a position of unencumbered *Being*. This is borne out by the explicit exploration on this subject in the section titled "A Good Name is Better Than Gold" in Elijah Muhammad's *Message to the Blackman*. Muhammad writes:

All nations of the earth are recognized by the name by which they are called. By stating one's name, one is able to associate an entire order of a particular civilization simply by name alone ...

It is only when we come to America and learn the names that our people are now going by that we discover that a whole nation of 20,000,000 black people are going by the names of white people ...

My poor blind, deaf and dumb people are going by the wrong names and until you accept the truth of your true identity and accept the names of your people and nation we will never be respected because of this alone. This is one of the reasons Almighty Allah has come among us, that is, to give us His Names, the Most Holy and Righteous Names of the Planet Earth ...

I warn you, my people, discard your former slave-master's names and be willing and ready to accept one of Allah's Pure and Righteous Names that He Alone will give our people from His Own Mouth! A good name is, indeed, better than gold.[12]

What we find in this quote is the foundation of Malcolm X's resistance to the effort by the interlocutors in the example examined here to establish a form of supremacy by requiring acknowledgment of what his religious practice has established as substantive disassociation from "civilization." This is the dialectical relationship to the claim expressed by Elijah Muhammad that by "...stating one's name, one is able to associate an entire order of a particular civilization simply by name alone..." What I mean here is that the acceptance and acknowledgment of the names imposed initially as a product of slave-making and maintaining them as a product of the erasure of identity that is the goal and effect of continued subjugation is the opposite of the project of reclamation of identity that is the goal presented by Muhammad. When confronted with a demand to acknowledge his slave name, Malcolm X cannot acquiesce, in that this practice is an existential threat to his positive reclamation of identity as an individual, as well as serving to undermine the entire political project established with this thinking. Malcolm X knows this, and I argue that the interlocutors here who serve as representatives of this logic as well as practitioners of its coercive effects know it as well. To the extent that the theological doctrine of the Nation of Islam is applied in the register of naming – and this is naming understood as the thick concept it represents for identity, possession, role and erasure of both historical and political context – the structures of power that benefit from this situation recognize the import and what it portends for their political project.

What is particularly interesting from a perspective of theology as it relates to the notion of the divine imperative of naming is the manner in which Muhammad's effort here tends to refuse Eden and the imprimatur of Adam by broadening this practice and its implication to allow the individual to serve in the position of "Name Giver par excellence." The theology here proposes that it is Elijah Muhammad who serves as a messenger to the people to notify them of their direct access to the positive Will of Allah with all that means from the perspective of theological and political practice. Muhammad writes: "I am naught but a warner and a Messenger to you, my people, not self-sent but sent directly from Almighty God (Allah)."[13] What is interesting here is that Muhammad does not take the responsibility of naming but authorizes the people to take the responsibility to name themselves. This is buttressed by the understanding that this divinely ordained resistance to the effort to harm the Black man by structures of white power will ultimately reveal the proper names.

The next step along this thinking is the general employment of the variable "X" in lieu of an "actual" name in most cases. This is implicative for viewing this practice through the theoretical lens of both Du Bois' "Second-Sight" and Fanon's "zone of non-being." This is again much about the possibility of using the thinking of Malcolm X as legible through these thinkers but perhaps more precisely to read them from the perspective of Malcolm. What this seems to mean is that all of these thinkers are aware of the refraction of the Cartesian *cogito* when it is applied to the self-awareness and possibility of recognition of figures who exist in this externally imposed state of subjective destruction. This is what is so critically important about the historical linkage Malcolm X emphasizes to his contemporary understanding of the loss of coherent genealogy to the ills of slavery. To approach this thinking through his engagement with the fracturing of the *cogito* for the subaltern figure renders self-reflection without context a process of ever-deepening forms of self-hatred: *I think therefore I hate myself.* This self-hatred is based upon a lack of context on the part of individuals that allows them to recognize that the knowledge that they have about the self is externally imposed. Until the subject realizes that the context of the depraved manner in which they perceive themselves is based upon layers of externally imposed narratives that recognize the subject as marginal, there is no manner in which self-reflection can resolve this problematic. Malcolm X is channeling, in ever more complex ways, the foundational understanding of the Nation of Islam that recognizes the erasure of both the historical as well as geo-political spatiality of the "Negro" in order to provide the impetus for the creation of technologies of self-(re)creation. Elijah Muhammad frames the depths of this process of self-misrecognition in terms of cognitive disability; "[m]y poor blind, deaf and dumb people." What this means in terms that are metaphysical rather than physical is that the subjects in question are shielded from cognition of their historical selves (broadly understood) and this shielding tends to reify a lack of positive understanding of the self that, in a process of circular logic, authorizes continued political marginalization. The subjects are meant to understand that they are suffering depraved political subjectivity because they are ineligible for full citizenship – because they do not deserve it. They do not deserve it because there has been an historical relationship to a lack of positive political subjectivity. This is substantively what is going on in the discourse between Malcolm X and O'Connor.

As mentioned previously, both O'Connor and Malcolm X are focused on genealogy: O'Connor is invested in requiring Malcolm X to acknowledge that he cannot distance himself from this logic. Malcolm X's position is that it is in the recognition of the genealogy of this naming that he finds the possibility of escaping its logic. This is what Du Bois describes as Second-Sight. Malcolm X understands the metaphysical trick that is embedded in accepting the possibility of being named by the other bent on defining political, social and economic boundaries in that process. The employment of "X" at this stage of this process is about creating a space of radical possibility that is not necessarily revealed or perhaps even defined. Naming, in the thinking of Malcolm X, is the first step in a process of positive recreation of identity. In fact, the naming positions itself at the beginning and ending of this political and metaphysical project through the reclamation of a self-authorized form of Adamic Naming that is based upon theologically authorized separation from the standards of constituted governmental authority.

The question here seems to be what we are to make of this notion of emptiness as exemplified by the "X" employed through much of Malcolm X's political career? It is perhaps interesting to consider this take on the explicit erasure of subject identity through the process of the transatlantic slave trade and colonialism in Africa against or perhaps through the Negritude movement. What I mean here is that in certain specific ways, the Nation of Islam eliminates what a thinker like Fanon understands to be the limits of Negritude because of the creation of particular forms of mythology that related colonized or diasporic people to African identity. This thinking is a forerunner to important elements of the Afrocentric movement. The Nation of Islam certainly establishes a linkage to non-Western ways of thinking if only through their employment of Islam as a theological and cultural tether to a notion of robust and self-authorizing African/Black identity. Further, the NoI has developed a clear mythology regarding the existence of white people as exemplified by the cosmology in Elijah Muhammad's text that proposes the following:

> They [the white race] are not hostile toward me because I am a Muslim and because I am teaching the true religion, Islam, to my people and the worship of the true and living God who is not a spook, but is flesh and blood (Allah).
>
> They are hostile against me and my followers because we are the Original Black Nation whom they were made to hate from the very beginning of their existence, 6,000 years ago.
>
> They were not made to love or respect any member of the darker nations, for they are by nature, as Almighty Allah has taught me, incapable of loving even themselves.[14]

Nation of Islam doctrine, with respect to identity, mythologizes the existence of white people as the necessary and sufficient condition for the establishment of the depraved projects of enslavement, genocide and colonialism as phenomena that are not socially constructed per se but rather the predictable result of the depraved ontology of whiteness. The truth of the harm done to Black people is, however, stranger than fiction, so mythologizing the facts was not necessary. What this allows is a coherent understanding of the political, social and economic impact of slavery and colonialism that leads to a form of identity alienation that is memorialized by the variable that makes an unequivocal statement of recognition of the terms of this diminution of consciousness, while leaving "space" for that vacuum to be filled with self-authorized identity. Awareness of the terms and conditions of depraved self-consciousness and the marking of that self-consciousness of no true self-consciousness exemplified by the "X" is to bridge the distance between Du Bois' Second-Sight and Fanon's "zone of non-being."

By resolving the relationship of the self to the self by situating a cypher as the vessel to hold the components of positive self-recognition, the soul is now able to employ the body as the vehicle for achieving positive political, social and economic existence.

2

The Body

The political philosophy of Malcolm X is a corporeal philosophical system primarily because its foundation is the recognition of phenotypic Blackness, or perhaps more carefully, phenotype at a discernible separation from whiteness, as itself the manifestation of the political. As was explored in the previous chapter, Malcolm X and the Nation of Islam's preoccupation with "naming" is ultimately a project of reclamation of positive identity as it relates to the sovereign potentiality of the "so-called" Negro. It is axiomatic in the thinking of Malcolm X that the Negro, as a political subject, is a creation of white supremacy ideologies that cover the body that happens to be Black in layers of subject (dis)forming notions.

The first of these typologies of disforming notion is that the body of the subject in question is recognized by the coercive threat of the state as being excluded from the understanding of being a *willful* political actor. I emphasize *willful* here because it is also true that the Negro, in the thinking of Malcolm X, is always already political and a political actor even in the absence of free will. The difference between a subject existing as a willful political actor and being an actor only in serving as the target for the coercive threat of the state is substantively the difference between being a political actor and an object of the political. What is important for the thinking of Malcolm X here is that to be an object of the political is to be useful to the system of recognized and legitimate power as mattering because you do not matter. The question for Malcolm X is how to recover the possibility of *willful* political activity from this reactionary stance, understanding that, as a practical matter, Black political thought in the Atlantic World is a reactionary system of thinking. I use the term here "reactionary" carefully. I am marshaling the term to speak of the cause and effect relationship between white supremacist ideology and thinking that has as its focus the recovery of positive Black identity. Here we witness the importance of enslavement for the thinking of Malcolm X that appeared explicitly in his rejection of Western naming practices that erase the relationship of the diasporic body to Africa through its relationship to the enslaved condition. This speaks to the importance of recognizing this subjective destruction as an essential element of the subject-disforming nature of white supremacy. These practices reify elements of Blackness deemed negative and obscure and/or erase positive aspects of genealogical relationship to Africa. It is the accumulation of these bodies to fuel the political project of white supremacy as an Atlantic World phenomenon that exists as the necessary precursor to the problematic of naming. For Malcolm X these bodies were stolen and then coerced into labor practices that left them demeaned as sovereign political actors. The imposition of names following the forcible extraction of the cultural referent from these bodies is an exemplar of the totality of the project at hand. These bodies, having been enslaved, then un-named, then re-named, finally find themselves victims of the vacillation of political will on the part of the state with respect to their existence as willful and recognized participants or "citizens". This thinking traces the historical trajectory from enslavement to the failure of Reconstruction followed by systemic segregation and Jim Crow that provides the context for the lived experience of Malcolm X. The corporeal foundation of this philosophical system is based on this logic generally in that the creation and maintenance of subaltern identity is a project of the state and for Malcolm X it is made particular through his embodied relationship with the coercive threat of policing. I mean to propose several things here.

First, if we allow ourselves to view the thought of Malcolm X as evolutionary: roughly from his Garveyite upbringing to his death as a Pan-Africanist philosopher of revolutionary politics, there is no time during that trajectory when this thinker was not engaged in a "physical way" with the institution of policing. What that means in this argument is that Malcolm X "understands" policing in a manner that only an "ex-convict" can understand it and my argument is that his disdain for the arrest as spectacle of the civil rights movement and further the political implication of police brutality as both a demonstration of the problem that preoccupies his thinking as well as the point of attack of his radical politics are fundamentally related to that phenomenological experience. The philosophical system of Malcolm X, in this argument, has as its central preoccupation the institution of policing in that the coercive power of the state creates the "Negroes" in question and that coercive power, in the absence of the enslaved condition, functions to continue to marginalize the political possibilities of these actors through the employment of police power.

It should not be ignored here that there are two instances of police brutality, one in Harlem and another in Los Angeles, that serve to establish the political power of Malcolm X within the Black community and as a discernibly independent actor from the NoI. The instance in Harlem establishes him as a thinker who will present direct resistance to police power and in the second instance, the break with Elijah Muhammad and the Nation of Islam is illustrated and exacerbated by his refusal to stay out of the conflict with police there. This conflict was particularly acute in the case of the death at the hands of the police of NoI officer Ronald Stokes. Manning Marable's gloss of the conflict is instructive. He writes in *Malcolm X: A Life of Reinvention*:

> At heart, the disagreement between Malcolm X and Elijah Muhammad went deeper than the practical question of how to respond to the Los Angeles police assault. Almost from the moment Muhammad had been informed about the raid and Stoke's death, he viewed the tragedy as stemming from a lack of courage by Mosque No. 27's members. "Every one of the Muslims should have died," he was reported to have said, "before they allowed an aggressor to come into their mosque."[1]

The Black body as a space of political activity, political thought, and the potential for political viability, for Malcolm X, becomes the locus of self-sovereignty at the moment of the willful practice of naming, and at that point of self-recognition and authorization is able to discern the terms and conditions of its place in the white supremacist social order. What Malcolm X asserts about this condition is that the coercive threat of the state frames the existence of all Black people in the United States, and with that understanding situates police brutality as the key to understanding and thus unraveling this condition. A familiar passage from his 1963 speech known as the "Message to the Grass Roots" is relevant here where he expresses the following: "When I was in prison, I read an article – don't be shocked when I say that I was in prison. You're still in prison. That's what American means: prison."[2] This is an important argument for understanding the linkage of Malcolm X's political thought to the question of colonialism, anti-colonialism, and the possibility of understanding the "so-called" Negro as living under the conditions of colonialism because of the existence of the United States as what he understands as a "police state." Here, Malcolm X is explicit in the arguments he presents on May 29, 1964, in response to a false story that gangs of Black Muslims are wandering New York City intending to kill and maim white people. The speech is known as "The Harlem 'Hate Gang' Scare" and includes the following articulation of this argument:

> If we're going to talk about police brutality, it's because police brutality exists. Why does it exist? Because our people in this particular society live in a police state. A black man in America lives in a police state. He doesn't live in a democracy, he lives in a police state. That's what it is, that's what Harlem is …
>
> They [Algerians] lived in a police state; Algeria was a police state. Any occupied territory is a police state; and that is what Harlem is. Harlem is a police state; the police in Harlem, their presence is like occupation forces, like an occupying army. They're not in Harlem to protect us, they're not in Harlem to look out for our welfare; they're in Harlem to protect the interests of the businessmen who don't even live there.[3]

What seems important to consider from this passage is the notion proposed by Malcolm X that police brutality is distinct from the institution of policing. This means that the institution of policing has the possibility, when it functions properly, to provide protection rather than situating itself as a strictly coercive force. Malcolm X notes that the inseparability of the institution of policing from brutality is a phenomenon that exists "[b]ecause our people in this particular society live in a police state." The police state, in the understanding of Malcolm X, is a coercive state of being that marginalizes certain political subjects, in this case the Black body, in order to maintain an exploitative system of economic extraction.

There is reason here to reflect on this seemingly tautological formulation as similar in important ways to the reflection on the relationship between race and economics in Frantz Fanon's *Wretched of the Earth*. Fanon proposes the following binary: "The cause is the consequence; you are rich because you are white, you are white because you are rich."[4] Malcolm X's formulation as it relates to police brutality and the creation of identity might be presented as: *You are brutalized by the police because you are the "so-called" Negro. You are the "so-called" Negro because you are brutalized by the police.* The action defines the subject and the subject's existence invites the action. It is the strident relationship between the racialized political subject and citizenship that requires the establishment of a coherent and predictable relationship to the "Law" that preoccupies this thinking on the part of Malcolm X. What this means is that there is an important distinction in this thinking between the law as an institution of social order and the maintenance of a coercive state of existence authorized and maintained by brutality. Malcolm X is explicit on this point in this same discussion:

> I'm not against law enforcement. You need laws to survive and you need law enforcement to have an intelligent peaceful society; but we have to live in these places and suffer the type of conditions that exist from officers who lack understanding and who lack any human feeling, or lack any feeling for their fellow human being ...[5]

Here we witness the logic proposed by Malcolm X. The sequentiality of subjection in this formulation, the "conditions" that "we have to suffer," are the product of police brutality. Police brutality, in this formulation, establishes the existence of particular subjects and then serves as the mechanism for the maintenance of that order. It is essential to grapple with this foundational formulation on the part of Malcolm X that proposes a red-line distinction between laws and a coherent existence within a political project of laws and something like police brutality that renders the relation of the subject to the law incoherent. What this creates with respect to corporeality is layers of the distinction from the "norm" for the Black body: separated from a coherent relationship to law and then separated from the body politic as a result of this initial separation that finds this condition authorized and maintained through unaccountable violence. This violence as a force of political constitution is productively understood in its relationship to Walter Benjamin's understanding of law-establishing and law-maintaining violence generally and further to recognize police violence (brutality) as both at the same time. Benjamin's conclusions regarding police violence find it to be unique from the other forms of violence in that its "... ignominy lies in the fact that in this authority the separation of law-making and law-preserving violence is suspended."[6]

In the philosophical system of Malcolm X, the embodiment of Blackness as the locus of political marginalization creates at least two political possibilities or requirements for the subject in question. The first is the reclamation of Blackness as a human status that yields coherent participation in political order whether that be as a subject internal to a functioning state or through international recognition as a sovereign actor under threat in its coincident spatiality. The first possibility here is related to Du Bois' explicit notion that once white people recognize that talent resides within Blackness, the Black body would find acceptance within the body politic as a political, social and economic actor. The second possibility does not rely upon positive recognition within the state that marginalizes the subject but in fact employs that subaltern status to create a type of transnational identity for this body under threat. This concept will be explored in depth later.

The first "possibility" speaks to the notion of "sweeping the board clean" in some respect by a national project that situates itself as linked to the coherent relationship of the Black body in question to a type of citizenship that provides the possibility of acceptably balancing "Duties and Rights" and being recognized as a citizen.

In grappling with this thinking it is productive to relate police violence as brutality to the question of "Duties and Rights" and the potential of balance. What I am arguing is that in this formulation by Malcolm X, police brutality is situated as the pivot point of a see-saw. To unpack this relationship, it is important to hold onto Malcolm X's understanding of the law as essential to a societal order and police brutality as fracturing that possibility, along with Benjamin's understanding from his canonical essay "Concerning Violence" while still understanding law enforcement, as an institution and practice, as essential.

If we understand the placement of the pivot point of a mechanical representation of Duties and Rights as situated at the midpoint between the two and, as such and understood as "Law" in the positive sense of the term, an "increase" in Duties triggers a commensurate "increase" in Rights (see Figure 1). What I mean to do here is think of Duties as acting in a vector downward and Rights reacting to that force in the opposite direction.

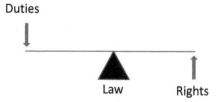

Duties

Law   Rights

Figure 1   Balanced Duties and Rights with laws enforced equitably

For instance, when this balance functions properly, a subject who extends some service to the state will have that sacrifice offset by a commensurate increase in Rights. An apparent example of this is the contemporary practice of boarding members of the armed forces first on US air carriers (see Figure 2).

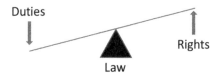

Figure 2   An increase in Duties causes an equal increase in Rights

Conversely, a decrease in Duties will trigger a predictable and proportionate decrease in Rights (see Figure 3).

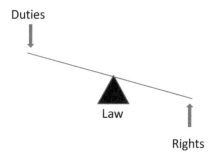

Figure 3   A decrease in Duties causes a proportionate decrease in Rights

If this pivot point is shifted from its midpoint and abandons the status of the law applied equally as expressed by Malcolm X, it is "shifted" by the force of police violence in the sense proposed by Benjamin in that it creates and maintains the law simultaneously. If this pivot point is located "closer" to the side of the mechanism that represents Duties, we find that small increases in Duties cause a disproportionate increase in Rights: this is effectively understood as Privilege. For instance, a white person might do something like walk into a church and execute nine Black people and when captured by the police be taken to a fast-food restaurant to get some lunch before being checked into the lock-up for fear that the killer might miss lunch service in jail (see Figure 4).

Conversely, to the extent that the pivot point is placed in this fashion, and there is an increase in Rights, it causes a disproportionately small

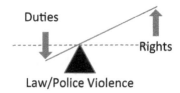

Figure 4 Decentering the pivot point toward Duties
causes a disproportionate increase in Rights; Privilege

increase in Duties. Again, this mechanically demonstrates privilege with
the notion of police violence "on the side" of Duty.

The displacement of the pivot point as a result of police violence closer
to the side of Rights mechanically demonstrates the status of marginalized subjectivity as a product of a disproportionate relationship between
Duties and Rights whereby small increases in Rights trigger a disproportionate increase in Duties. In this example, a young Black child, we might
imagine, could be playing with a toy gun in a state that grants people the
right to carry firearms openly, but be shot to death by the police (see
Figure 5).

Figure 5 Decentering the pivot point toward Rights causes a
disproportionate increase in Duties: Marginalized Subjectivity

An excerpt from a speech given by Malcolm X on April 27, 1962, about
a police killing in Los Angeles might productively be reviewed with the
theoretical lens presented here. Malcolm proposed the following:

> Once the police have convinced the white public that the "So-called"
> Negro community is a criminal element they can go in and question,
> brutalize, murder, unarmed innocent Negroes and the white pop-
> ulation is gullible enough to back them up. This makes the Negro
> community a police state. This makes the Negro neighborhood a
> police state. It's the most heavily patrolled. It has more police in it than
> any other neighborhood yet it has more crime in it than any other
> neighborhood. How can you have more cops and more crime? Why?
> It shows that the cops must be in cahoots with the criminals.[7]

Malcolm X here retreads his argument regarding the nature of police brutality that creates the Black community as a police state, but by thinking about this formulation from a perspective of the Duties and Rights binary elaborated here, and its relationship to police brutality, we are able to identify this mechanical relationship in the philosophical system he is presenting. If we situate being "Unarmed" and "Innocent" as Duties of the citizen, we would expect, in a political environment where the law functions properly, that these individuals have the commensurate "Right" to relief from unaccountably applied coercive force. What Malcolm X proposes here is that "unarmed" and "innocent" Negroes are subject to be "question[ed], brutalize[d], and murder[ed]" by the police, demonstrating that compliance with the Duty to follow the law does not come with the commensurate Right to protection from coercive force. It is, in fact, just the opposite and is further exacerbated by the fact that the "gullible" white community believes this is proper. What this further demonstrates is that Malcolm X understands the institution of policing generally and police brutality specifically as existing as exceptional from a white community that understands its operation through two essential mechanisms: first, the media and second, the acceptance that the "so-called" Negro, is best understood as representative of a negative, "criminal" element and therefore not eligible for full citizenship.

The corporeal relationship to this thinking needs to be made explicit. Malcolm X understands that racism is a product of the relationship of white supremacy to the "Other" which seems to amount to the necessity of having an allegedly sub-human foil in order to make explicit the hierarchical relationship of whiteness to Blackness. Much of this is related to points raised in the ontology chapter, where Nation of Islam orthodoxy regards Caucasians as sub-human subjects who marginalize the Black body in order to elevate their own status as Caucasians. This process is a profoundly violent one that chastises the body with physical and metaphysical violence that is designed to assure the subject of its subaltern status. The demi-citizen status of this subject renders this corporeal imperative on the part of chastiser and chastised the central point of conflict. This requires some elaboration.

Recall, Malcolm X sees the body of the "so-called" Negro as a political space. This space has boundaries like those of the geographic space of the post-Westphalian nation-state and the central problematic of this element of his system (prior to an exploration of the geographic spatiality in the next chapter) is for the bodies in question to resolve the force

exerted upon their being. There is a way in which the preceding discussion on Naming situates the practice all the way down as becoming
"corporeal" in the sense that the cipher of the variable allows the body
to resituate the constituting violence of subjective establishment through
loss into this vacant space to allow it the possibility of self-reflection
outside of the context of violence through subjective marginalization.

If we imagine the force exerted on these bodies as "filling" them to the
point of indistinction between the violence visited on the body and the
body/vessel itself, we can begin to understand that negative presupposi-
tions regarding Blackness overwhelm the body that is Black. Violence,
particularly that of the state in the form of police brutality, is the force
that fills this body that Malcolm X endeavors to evacuate and also render
impermeable to further attacks. As mentioned in the previous chapter,
the variable "X" serves to mark both the unknown and the space of possibility. Employing this understanding in the realm of corporeality, the
X can be understood to mirror the corporeal body and serve, first, as a
locus for the redirection of primarily metaphysical violence away from
the body that is Black. This allows a willful "twinning" of the Black body
that is fraught with possibility when understood to exist as a step beyond
Du Bois' tripartite understanding that expresses Two-ness (Negro and
American) as incompatible ways of being contained in the Black body.
Malcolm X productively advances this thinking.

At the level of the Negro in the dialectical relationship between Negro
and American, Malcolm X understands the "X" as a twinning of the
Negro, rendering this relationship within the Black body as composed
of the Negro-X opposed to the American. The argument advanced here
is that Malcolm X is situating an idealized existence within this corporeality that becomes the locus of the struggle for possession of this Black
body. The argument can proceed in several directions.

One proposal for unpacking this understanding is to imagine that the
resistance to acknowledging the relationship between the person known
as Malcolm Little and the renamed Malcolm X is to build an ideological
firewall between these fraught and, in many respects, oppositional ways
of being. By refusing the linkage between his body, the name Malcolm
Little for that body, and the possibility of the "X", Malcolm subverts the
Du Boisian opposition between American and Negro and establishes,
first, a coherent relationship between the Black body and positive
Blackness represented by the variable, while eliding the continued
practical existence of the Negro. The second stage in this thinking seems

to reside in maintaining the "X" as an effect of the cause of the violence of the creation of the Negro but fraught with possibility in its distinction from that ontology in no small part because of its lack of external definition. This leaves the Negro where it stands and allows it to remain as the target for the brutality of the state. Through an almost Zen-like project of self-affirmation in the face of the physical and metaphysical violence dedicated to erasing the "X" and reconstituting the hierarchical nature of the Negro–American binary, Malcolm X practices resistance through the repetition of the mantra that asserts over and over the separation of his corporeal existence from that of the Negro.

Again, Malcolm X appears to be positing an important re-reading of the Cartesian *cogito* from the perspective of the "so-called" Negro specifically and the "Other" generally. The first step in this process is recognition of the terms and conditions of the coercive context of white supremacy in which the "so-called" Negro exists that, up until the moment of self-recognition, prevented this subject from thinking about the self on the self's own terms. What this amounts to is avoiding confusing external marginalization as primary knowledge. The framework here is perhaps productively illuminated by examining elements of Jean-Paul Sartre's *Transcendence of the Ego*, in order to understand the fracturing of self-reflection through modes of externally imposed "confusion." The process described by Sartre begins with what he labels "consciousness in the first degree" or "unreflected consciousness."[8] As Sartre theorizes this foundational step in the process of consciousness, the inapplicability of it to the status of Malcolm X's "so-called" Negro makes itself plain.

> We should add that this consciousness of consciousness – except in the case of reflective consciousness which we shall dwell on later – is not *positional*, which is to say that consciousness is not for itself its own object. Its object is by nature outside of it, and that is why consciousness *posits* and *grasps* the object in the same act. Consciousness knows itself only as absolute inwardness. We shall call such a consciousness: consciousness in the first degree, or *unreflected* consciousness.[9]

Malcolm X, by grounding his thinking on the corporeal, witnesses the abuse of the Black body as militating against the Sartrean notion of unreflected consciousness as "absolute inwardness" in that this subjective creation through police violence obviously requires interaction among different actors. This can be articulated by proposing that the subject that preoccupies Malcolm X, which is similar in important ways to Du Bois' subject, is not capable of unreflected consciousness and exists without the possibility of "consciousness in the first degree." This condition has dire consequences for the *cogito* of this figure, which suffers a condition Sartre describes as "reflective consciousness."[10] Sartre, in working through this thinking, demonstrates a separation between the *cogito* of Husserl and the Cartesian understanding that I propose opens the breach for Malcolm X to theorize the existence of this fragmented subjectivity along with modes of dismantling this circumstance. Sartre writes:

> A pure consciousness is an absolute quite simply because it is conscious of itself. It remains therefore a "phenomenon" in the very special sense in which "to be" and "to appear" are one. It is all lightness, all translucence. This it is which differentiates the *Cogito* of Husserl from the Cartesian *Cogito*. But if the *I* were a necessary structure of consciousness, this opaque *I* would at once be raised to the rank of an absolute. We would then be in the presence of a monad. And this, indeed, is unfortunately the orientation of the new thought of Husserl. Consciousness is loaded down; consciousness has lost that character which rendered it the absolute existent *by virtue of non-existence*. It is heavy and *ponderable*. All the results of phenomenology begin to crumble if the *I* is not, by the same title as the world, a relative existent; that is to say, an object *for* consciousness.[11]

This notion of consciousness being an object for itself is the linchpin in developing an understanding of the theory of consciousness that is foundational to the philosophical system of Malcolm X. This thinking, through Sartre, allows a richer reading of this notion of "love and understanding" that haunts the thinking of Fanon in *Black Skin, White Masks*, which is useful in unpacking the thought of Malcolm X. The process of consciousness on the part of the "so-called" Negro is predicated on the internalization of the abjection that becomes the content of a misapprehension of Du Bois' Second-Sight or/and Fanon's "series of emotional aberrations" as consciousness in the first degree when it is actually a reflected, interactive and coercive brand of secondary consciousness. This creates a point of ontological *mis-re-memory* in that the subject perceives an *I* that is positioned as the foundation of consciousness that is supposed to be unreflected consciousness but is, in fact, reflected consciousness. Sartre makes the important point that "all writers who have described the *Cogito* have dealt with it as a reflective operation, that is to say, an operation of the second degree."[12]

Carefully unpacking this, we find that Sartre proposes that the *cogito* is in fact the synthesis of two consciousnesses:

> … an indissoluble unity of the reflecting consciousness and the reflected consciousness (to the point that the reflecting consciousness could not exist without the reflected consciousness). But the fact remains that we are in the presence of two consciousnesses, one which is conscious of the other.[13]

This would, if it were the crux of the matter, render American consciousness, which I situate as the object for examination with the Sartrean tool, in that, in the political formulation relevant to Malcolm X, it serves as the normative condition, as fundamentally at odds with the type of consciousness of the Negro subject that is most thoroughly described by Du Bois' tripartite formulation. The separation between the two subjects, American and Negro, at the level of the *cogito* is thrown back to the point of departure which, for the former, is true consciousness in the first degree and, for the latter, is consciousness in the second degree mistaken for consciousness in the first degree. Sartre incisively brings into the conversation, returning to the consciousness of the *I*, the *I* that thinks, and proposes that:

> … the consciousness which says *I Think* is precisely not the consciousness which thinks. Or rather it is not *its own* thought which it posits as this thetic act. We are then justified in asking ourselves if the *I* which thinks is common to the two superimposed consciousnesses, or if it is not rather the *I* of reflected consciousness. All reflected consciousness is, indeed, in itself unreflected, and a new act of the third degree is necessary in order to posit it. Moreover, there is no infinite regress here, since a consciousness has no need at all of a reflecting consciousness in order to be conscious of itself. It simply does not posit itself as an object.[14]

The situation for the Negro subject is related to the interaction of the two reflected consciousnesses, one of which, the American, meets the strictures posed here by Sartre, while the other, the Negro, does not. In substance, the notion of the superimposition of the two consciousnesses fails here in that Negro consciousness is not "true self-consciousness" in that, contrary to Sartre's account, this form of consciousness has a need for reflect(ed)ive consciousness and is in fact "only" that reflected consciousness. It, "Negro consciousness," is incapable of *not* "posit[ing] itself as an object." Hence the necessity of Malcolm X employing the "X" as a "new act of the third degree," in the Sartrean sense, that posits a new cognitive relationship between the Black body and its metaphysical reflection upon itself at the level of first-degree awareness of the self.

What is essential here is to understand that Malcolm X has no intention of allowing the Black body to be absorbed by the "X" and essentially disappear as the frame of reference for this form of subjective existence. On the contrary, he is emphasizing the social fact that the non-existent Negro has been situated as the stand-in for the true corporeality of the Black body. This is explicit in the work of Du Bois framed here as essential to this understanding that designates the Black body as distinct from the Negro. What Malcolm X's philosophical system endeavors to accomplish is the absorption of the Negro into the "X" for all of the essential historical relevance to the construction of Black identity, while allowing the body to stand as its own point of reference in the assemblage of this new political and social subjectivity. Malcolm X's focus, to the point of fracturing his relationship with the Nation of Islam, on the societal ill of police violence, is to recognize the coercive force's role in preventing the reconstruction of the physical space of the Black body as a positive, self-referential political space that can be included in the calculation of a political and social project that recognizes that same body as an accepted and acceptable political actor. Violence by the state, to the extent that it is rewarded through a lack of accountability to the laws designed to prevent it, is deleterious to this project. So long as the Black body is the target of police brutality, and this brutality needs to be understood as it must be now as inclusive of the failure to hold the purveyor legally responsible for the transgression, the Negro overwhelms the political space of the Black body and becomes the self-referential and self-reifying fact of political marginalization.

In substance this elevation of the Black body as a positive political space represents, arguably, the locus of the continued relevance of the thought of Malcolm X across time and space and various radical political traditions. What I mean by this is that the beauty of Blackness in the face of coercive threat, not just at the level of the aesthetic (and this "just" is to differentiate, not to render hierarchical), but as political possibility in the face of threats to render it if not marginal then inert, is an ethic that elevates Blackness as the font of possibility for a form of political project that transcends race through its reaffirmation in a mode of understanding that rejects the understanding of race in the Western tradition as an ordering principle for purposes of creating the subaltern as the foundation of projects that use it as the base upon which they construct "Identity in Opposition." This is arguably the result of the phenomenology of Malcolm X, made explicit in his return from the Hajj, that witnesses his refutation of the strict understanding of race as speaking to rigid notions of political possibility or existential threat. Malcolm X penned the following in his diary on Friday, April 17, 1964, that speaks to this point.

> Friday 17th of April
> [Saudi Arabia]
> El Jumah prayers: crowded, all colors, bowing in unison – not conscious of color (race) around whites for 1st time in my life. The whites don't seem white – Islam actually removed differences – Persian (white) followed me around, offering the hospitality of eating with his family – pilgrims from Nigeria & Ghana, very vocal & confident.[15]

Recall the earlier argument that proposed that Malcolm X as a thinker, in contradistinction to the written archive of most philosophers in the Western tradition, is primarily understood through his discourse. Along with that formulation there is further a corporeal element to this thinking that bears analysis. It is not just the complex understanding of the spectacle of the Black body in spaces and places that Malcolm X translates into a form of politics in and of itself, but also the photographic archive of Malcolm himself as well as his careful thinking around coercive force and the Black body that preoccupies this examination. There are two photographs rendered here (see Figures 6 and 7) that attract my attention because of their possibility for furthering our understanding of essential elements of this philosophical system.

There are many options in the photographic archive of Malcolm X that are available to stand in as the object for philosophical analysis: the mug shot of the recently-arrested Malcolm Little comes to mind. There is the thoughtful Malcolm, peering into the camera through horn-rimmed glasses as if to demand of his interlocutors an accounting of themselves beyond the four corners of their debate. There is the iconic Malcolm X behind a podium with his finger pointing into space and his mouth seeming to form the hard-formed "F." Of course, one should never forget Malcolm X peering out of his window brandishing a rifle: an image ready-made for his assertion that he would seek freedom "By Any Means Necessary." There are also the images of Malcom with Martin Luther King, Malcolm praying in Saudi Arabia, Malcolm with Elijah Muhammad, Castro, Redd Foxx or Maya Angelou. All of the images individually, and the archive collectively, are rich, but it is this image of Malcolm X and the newly-minted heavyweight champion of the world, the then Cassius Clay, that draws my attention first (see Figure 6).

Figure 6   Muhammad Ali and Malcolm X
(Bob Gomel/Sygma, via Getty Images)

There are the obvious elements of time and space that must be accounted for here. Figure 6 is one of a series of photographs taken of the celebration at the diner in the Hampton House Hotel in Miami, hours after Cassius Clay's unexpected defeat of Sonny Liston on February 24, 1964. Before addressing the central figures in this image – teacher and pupil, watcher and watched, photographer and photographed – the room must be examined from the periphery inward, to witness the performance of radical political subjectivity expressed here.

There appear to be three white men in the scene, one in a suit and horn-rimmed glasses, his eyes focused away from the subjects of the photograph and his comportment disorientated. In the world assembled here and memorialized in the photograph, the white man has been pushed to the periphery, even here at this lunch counter, which has been altered from its employment as the locus of dehumanizing coercive threat to the Black body. The notion that Black people could occupy the lunch counter in this fashion, while pushing white men to the periphery, is emblematic of the performance of the philosophical system in this space. Additionally, the center of gravity of the scene is Cassius Clay and Malcolm X – not a white man.

To the right of this first white man, and against the wall, is another white man who appears to be an employee of the diner. The logic of this inversion of the racial hierarchy continues here in that, in contradistinction to the images of diner employees expelling Black bodies from lunch counters or denying them service, this individual is pushed as far from the counter as possible and seems to be engaged in serving a room full of African–Americans who have "Blackened" the space. The third white man is in uniform. A police officer is here and his kinetic coercive threat has been overwhelmed and decentered.

The next figure that attracts my attention in the same photograph is the Black woman, here in this profoundly gendered space. It is not news that the Nation of Islam operates under the debilitating regime of patriarchy. This woman is one who has resisted exclusion from this space and this embodied presence must be marked for its importance in its singularity. She appears determined to move to the center of the action. This situation of being present yet decentered, as captured in the photograph, exemplifies the troubling legacy of misogyny that must be interrogated in this system of thought. This gendered body finds itself singular and decentered in the dominant, Black, male phantasm that characterizes much of the thinking of Malcolm X.

bell hooks, in the essay, "Malcolm X: The Longed-for Feminist Manhood," asserts that, at least when *Outlaw Culture: Resisting Representation* was first published, in 1994, "[c]ritical scholarship on Malcolm X contains no *substantial* work from a feminist standpoint."[16] Both hooks, in the essay referred to, and Clenora Hudson-Weems, in a 1993 journal article, "From Malcolm Little to El Hajj Malik El Shabazz: Malcolm's Evolving Attitude Toward Africana Women," insist that the thinking of Malcolm X has to be examined against the evolution of a personal biography that, at the end, seemed to embrace the role of women in the liberation struggle. Hudson-Weems writes:

He evolved to the realization that the freedom, growth and development of Africana women were an integral part of Africana people's freedom the world over. Unlike the emphasis of so-called "Black feminist," who focuses on the plight of Black women within the context of feminist theory, Malcolm, during his last stage of development, focused on the family.[17]

There is little doubt that "Detroit Red," the Malcolm who ended up in prison for burglary and conducted abusive relationships with women that were often complicated by race, can never be understood as representative of a positive relationship with anything that approximates feminism. In spite of this truth, hooks proposes that this transition from what can be understood as depraved misogyny to something that approximates a proto-feminist stance, must be considered, writing:

> The truth is, despite later changes in his thinking about gender issues, Malcolm's earlier public lectures advocating sexism have had a much more powerful impact on black consciousness than the comments he made during speeches and interviews towards the end of his life which showed a progressive evolution in his thinking on sex roles. This makes it all the more crucial that all assessments of Malcolm's contribution to black liberation struggle emphasize this change, not attempting in any way to minimize the impact of his sexist thought but rather to create a critical climate where these changes are considered and respected, where they can have a positive influence on those black folks seeking to be more politically progressive.[18]

The photograph that demands our attention here is caught between these two extremes. Malcolm X's relationship with the Nation of Islam had witnessed the abandonment of his former virulent and dangerous brand of sexism for what can most charitably be described as patronizing and paternalistic. Here, Malcolm X has constructed the type of black and male environment that NoI orthodoxy understood to be the vehicle toward something like positive radicalism. hooks understands this ideology, as the notion that "... the institutionalization of black male patriarchy is ... the answer to our problems."[19] The Black woman is present here in this photograph and this imaginary, but Malcolm X has not reached the point of reconciling the patriarchy that infects his thinking with reality. His appearance with Fannie Lou Hamer in December of

1964 sees Malcolm X making a public statement that complicates this paternalism toward women by understanding them as having a role in the revolution but also as the bearers of culture in the sense that they care for children. In his engagement with Hamer, he strikes a different note, but still affirms the notion that Black men are responsible for Black women in ways that can be understood as patriarchal and demeaning. In the appearance with Hamer, Malcolm X proposes the following:

> When I listen to Mrs. Hamer, a black woman – could be my mother, my sister, my daughter – describe what they had done to her in Mississippi, I ask myself how in the world can we ever expect to be respected as *men* when we allow something like that to be done to our women and we do nothing about it?[20]

First, we have to mark the paternalistic speech and the notion, at least implicitly, that women somehow belong to men and are part of a relationship to the protection of property that does violence to the idea of radical and egalitarian humanism. Working from that understanding, the notion of inherent and logical disrespect as an effect of not being able to protect property speaks to the specter of humiliation that hangs over the thinking of Malcolm X. It is not just that the man is not respected or is not in a position to respect himself or be respected by "his" woman. It is also the implicit understanding that the white supremacist is invested in a project of humiliating the maligned Other at the level of the foundation of their familial relationships.

Orlando Patterson exposes this in his tripartite understanding of the enslaved condition that, in addition to being a product of being allowed to live and serve as a "substitute for death in war"[21] also featured "natal alienation"[22] and, with respect to this notion of humiliation, "persons who had been dishonored in a generalized way."[23] Malcolm X understands the crisis under which a figure like Fannie Lou Hamer operates as a form of dishonor that is only exacerbated by the inability of the "man" to do anything about it. At this stage of his thinking, Malcolm X is struggling to reconcile patriarchy with his acknowledgment that "... Hamer [is] one of the country's foremost freedom fighters."[24] hooks understands this as a progression in his thinking that is borne out of two related events: his awareness of the sexual harassment of women within the NoI by Elijah Muhammad and, because of that break, the need to "build an autonomous constituency."[25] It is telling that the breach with the NoI came, in large measure, because of Malcolm's refusal to accept the male prerogative to women's bodies that was exemplified by the predatory behavior of Muhammad. Following hooks, there is no reason not to believe that "[h]ad he lived, Malcolm might have explicitly challenged sexist thinking in as adamant a manner as he had advocated it."[26]

Understanding this, and returning to Figure 6 as text, it is the notion of humiliation at the hands of white supremacy that renders the subject of this photograph so potent a symbol and realization of the philosophical system of Malcolm X.

There is little argument that Malcolm X and Cassius Clay, soon to declare himself Cassius X, prior to being re-re-named Muhammad Ali by Elijah Muhammad in order to fracture the relationship between Malcolm X and the boxer, are the primary subjects of this photograph. Before dealing with the principal subjects in the photo it is important to understand what Malcolm X is doing here in the first place. The argument is that in many ways his preoccupation with the sport of boxing illustrates important elements of the essential corporeality of his philosophical system. The 2016 text, *Blood Brothers: The Fatal Friendship Between Malcolm X and Muhammad Ali*, by Randy Roberts and Johnny Smith, essentially proposes (as the title implies) that there was a fundamental toxicity to this relationship. What these authors assert is that Malcolm X was interested in using his relationship with Ali as a shield against attack by the Nation of Islam.[27] I am not so interested in the ins and outs of that proposition but rather the understanding of physicality in American societal order generally, and with respect to the Black community and the Nation of Islam particularly, that render it possible plausibly to propose that a boxer could shield an activist of the stature of Malcolm X from threat.

What Muhammad Ali represents, ideologically, for the philosophical system of Malcolm X, is an affirmation of the Black body as powerful, beautiful and, most particularly, with respect to Ali, able to protect its independence with physical strength. With this understanding it is particularly interesting to trace the political corporeality of Muhammad Ali as demonstrative of the possibility of resistance to the kinetic threat of state violence.

Our sports culture has witnessed a profound decline in the stature of boxing generally and the heavyweight championship specifically. In the moment that preoccupies our attention, the heavyweight champion of the world was generally regarded as the most important athlete on planet

Earth and along with that comes a profoundly nationalist element of that understanding. The heavyweight champion becomes representative of the physical potentiality of a nation-state and this linkage is particularly fraught when the Black body comes to represent the potentiality of the state that has created it as the marginalized and maligned Negro. What I explore here is the manner in which the physicality of Muhammad Ali fractures the coercive logic of the marginalized self-consciousness exposed by Du Bois that renders Negro and American as incompatible subjectivities. As mentioned above, Malcolm X endeavors to resolve this tension by establishing the "X" as something of a "relief valve" from which to establish alternatives modes of relational political subjectivity both inter- and intrasubjectively. Ali, as heavyweight champion of the world, expands this logic. Malcolm X is explicit in an interview following the defeat of Sonny Liston by the then Cassius Clay declaring:

> And now here comes Cassius. The exact contrast of everything that was representative of the Negro image. He said he was the greatest. All of the odds were against him and he upset the odds makers. He won. He became victorious. He became the champ.[28]

What I mean here is that the notion that the heavyweight champion and American are ideally linked is complicated by the appearance of the Black body as champion and therefore representative of the state. Malcolm X, in concert with Ali, require the logic of white supremacy and nationalism to account for the political sovereignty of the Black body by disallowing the Blackness to be overwhelmed by the heavyweight champion-ness.

What happens here, mechanically, is that from the perspective of the normative American invested in the maintenance of white supremacy, the Black heavyweight champion is intellectually separated from the mass of Black people and becomes exceptional and therefore acceptable to the body politic. In this case, Muhammad Ali (*né* Cassius Clay, *né* Cassius X), following the philosophical understanding of Malcolm X for the creation of self-referential political sovereignty, refuses this erasure through cooption of his Blackness by taking on the "X" to reify his Blackness, the sense of loss at the hands of white supremacy, and most importantly, the control of his horizon of possibility through his own will and most importantly the beauty of Blackness in rejection of white supremacist logic. This is an argument for the philosophical importance of the relationship between Malcolm X and Muhammad Ali that does not require us to linger on arguments about the toxicity of that union proposed by the authors of *Blood Brothers*. This image speaks to this philosophical argument.

It is of course appropriate to observe that Malcolm X, uncharacteristically, is not the center of attention in this environment and does not appear to be desirous of being so. For a moment we can suspend the facts surrounding the production of this image and imagine that the only photographer is Malcolm X and not Howard L. Bingham, Ali's personal photographer, who documents the documenter. Malcolm X is recognized as a subject who understood the power of photography both in front of and behind the camera. Maurice Berger draws attention to this in his 2012 article, "Malcolm X as Visual Strategist," where he proposes:

> A keen steward of the Nation of Islam's visual representation, Malcolm X often carried a camera, his way of "collecting evidence," as Gordon Parks once observed. He relied on photographs to provide the visual proof of Black Muslim productivity and equanimity that sensationalistic headlines and verbal reporting often negated. When photojournalists visited the community, he tried to steer them toward the kinds of affirmative images – shots of contented family life, children at play and school, and thriving businesses and institutions – that might subtly ameliorate the negative texts that he knew would inevitably accompany them.[29]

This image of Malcolm X capturing an image is properly understood as an important aspect of this archival project, this collection of "evidence" that I am situating as an essential element of his philosophical praxis. The evidence presented here picks up the extension of the theory of subjectivity proposed by Du Bois while at the same time documenting the "affirmative" elements that Berger establishes. What is being documented here is related to my earlier assertion that Malcolm X understands the body as a political space and as such, particularly as it relates to the recovery of individual sovereignty under conditions of coercive threat, a political institution and, in the case of Ali, also a "thriving business." The profound influence on Cassius Clay in his progress to becoming the political institution of Muhammad Ali is both begun and fulfilled in this moment following the victory over Sonny Liston, a representative of a particular type of Blackness that is "out" in a different and more acceptable way than the "out-ness" promoted by Malcolm X. To put it plainly and perhaps reductively: Ali is a "bad nigger" in a completely different fashion than Sonny Liston. What Malcolm X is documenting here is the possibility of spatial transformation by Black bodies that trends toward political viability versus reaffirmation of political marginalization and social pathology. Malcolm X's apparent pleasure at the moment is written in the smile (mischievous?) on his face as he interacts with the beaming Ali. They share a secret and the notion that the world will soon be hip to it speaks to the possibility of an expansion of the horizon of possibility of this political project beyond the geographic space of this hotel diner in the moments following a major athletic victory.

Ali owns this moment as he always did, even in relationship to the massive presence of Malcolm X. Outside of the obvious fact that the newly-crowned heavyweight champion of the world is the man of the hour, it is the realization or embodiment of the bifurcation of the Negro from the Black body to be replaced with physical and metaphysical mastery of the self that seems relevant here. What is clear from this photograph is that these two men, Malcolm X and Muhammad Ali, have created, *in situ*, a uniquely black and empowered space but, with the exception of the woman mentioned above, an all-male space, a phenomenon that requires us to take up the question of gendered bodies in this philosophical system. Malcolm X is preternaturally concerned with the plight of Black women in a societal order dedicated to marginalizing racialized bodies, but prior to taking the next step in considering this system of thought we have to deal with the inevitable destruction of the Black body. This phantasm cannot hold.

In Figure 7, the decentering of the police power of the state that attends the visual tableau in the diner that served as the spatial manifestation of the political philosophy of Malcolm X has been fractured. Here, the broken body of Malcolm X has been surrounded by the very power that he opposed and worked his entire public life to resist. One can almost imagine the possibility of erasing everything that occurred between that evening at the Hampton House on February 24, 1964, and the assassination of Malcolm X at the Audubon Ballroom on February 21, 1965. There is reason to do so. Malcolm's corporeality could not hold itself within that phantasm for a full year and, in spite of all the motion between those two moments, the specter of death and violence

Figure 7   Malcolm X on Stretcher After Shooting (Bettmann, via Getty Images)

that haunts the thought of Malcolm X arrives to dismantle the idealized environment he imagined to refute it.

In this image, the Black body that had formed a field of physical and intellectual protection around the reverie of Malcolm and Cassius has been shattered. It is not necessary to rehearse the series of betrayals, agents, double agents, threats and conspiracies made real that enabled the body of Malcolm X to be broken in this fashion. This is ably handled in other spaces. What preoccupies my attention here is the fact that the body of Malcolm X that had banished the subject dys-forming presence. The police are understood to treat Black people in a way that renders them sub-human. I am reminded here of Jean-Luc Nancy's examination of the image of the newly-risen Christ interacting with Magdalene in his text *Noli me Tangere: On the Raising of the Body*.[30] In that text, Nancy asserts the import of the manner in which Christ forbids Mary from touching his body because he is on the way to his Father.

This image throws us back to the beginning of Malcolm X's understanding of the circular logic of Negro-ness and its relationship to police brutality. The fact that Malcolm X's body has to be removed from the killing field by those he despised most speaks to the necessity of the completion of his system in order to render it functional. The fantastic spatiality of the Hampton Inn was buttressed against the overwhelming context of the coercive threat to Black bodies. Harlem, as a geographic space, at this time, offers no such protection and without the resolution of the journey to revolutionary alteration of the contexts of existence, Malcolm must die and in that death underscores the necessity to translate this imaginary into reality through a relationship to geography.

3

Geographic Space

To be clear about what is at stake here, and the reason I have elected to end the previous chapter on Malcolm X's employment of the body in his system with the corporeal death of Malcolm X, is to ensure that we keep track of the complication of sequentiality that haunts projects of radical political change. To be direct, the problem is illustrated by the fact that one must decide upon the imperative of radical social change before enacting radical social change. In the case of the subjects that concern Malcolm X, the endeavor to alter the way the Self regards the Self sends shockwaves through the structure of white supremacy that has situated the demeaned self-regard of the diasporic Black person as the primary mechanism for the maintenance of systems of oppression. For white supremacy to witness scenes like the one we have examined in Hampton House is to witness what they understand as an act of revolutionary violence in the sense that Benjamin understands violence that fractures existing legal structures and establishes a new regime of law.

We have witnessed, in our contemporary moment, as a result of the omnipresence of camera phones that allow the capture of even the most mundane and quotidian moments, Black people facing physical assault and/or confrontation from the police for merely occupying space in a manner that implies personal sovereignty. The subject that begins to reestablish personal subjectivity through the process of addressing the ontological self, causes the corporeal self to become unstable and unable to exist safely in real space. White supremacy, as a project, avails itself of this disorientation and arrests the forward progress before the subject can establish a stable, geographically-discernible platform. With this in mind, the materiality of the philosophical system of Malcolm X demands consideration of the next step beyond the body, which is to wrestle with his understanding of the primacy of geographic spatiality. The most important reason for unpacking this conceptualization of geographic spatiality and its relationship to politics generally, and Black radical politics specifically, is ultimately to understand the complex nature of Malcolm X's notion of Black Nationalism. As I proposed in the introduction to this book, there is a way in which the thinking of Malcolm X with respect to spatiality is profoundly *transnational* as well as *"quasi-terrestrial."* The first of these terms, "transnational," is fairly straightforward; it is the second term that I have derived for purposes of this thinking that requires explanation before proceeding further and addressing the first term more carefully.

As a point of departure, the philosophical system that we are exploring understands that the locus of the marginalization of Black bodies is a product of a system of oppression that has, at its roots, the land theft and genocide that provides for the spatial existence of the New World. Malcolm X understands that the coterminus crimes against humanity of the genocide of indigenous people and the enslavement of people of African descent creates the possibility of the political project that creates the Negro and is necessarily the system that must be dismantled. What this means is that a political project, and the philosophical system that drives it, designed to establish identity in the space that has created the subaltern subject, must comprehensively deal with geography. This presents at least two "irreducible difficulties," in the parlance of James Baldwin. The first of these is that the marginalization of Black bodies is a global project of existential harm. The second is that bodies, political or otherwise (recall my proposition that Malcolm X understands the Black body to be a "political space"), require a physical place to gather and fulfill the logic of their political subjectivity. This means that Malcolm X, from an ethical standpoint, is not interested in projects of displacement of others in order to establish a geographic national identity because, as a practical matter, there is frankly no room on planet Earth for a "new" political project. Therefore some new understanding of the relationship of geography to politics is required. The final chapter of this text will take up Malcolm X's conceptualization of revolution, but internal to that thinking is the imperative of land. In the 1963 speech known as "The Message to the Grass Roots," Malcolm X proposes the following:

Look at the American Revolution in 1776. That revolution was for what? For land. Why did they want land? Independence. How was it carried out? Bloodshed. Number one, it was based on land, the basis of independence. And the only way they could get it was bloodshed. The French Revolution – what was it based on? The landless against the landlord. What was it for? Land. How did they get it? Bloodshed.[1]

An important note to understand in this statement is that violence, as such, is not an abstract concept or based upon a need for revenge, but strictly a means to the political necessity of radical landed-ness as the foundation of independence. This will be explored in some detail in the next part of this chapter, but we witness here the double-bind of the need for land and the need for violence and even death to serve the movement to acquire it. I cannot locate support for the notion in the political system of Malcolm X that conquest is either feasible or ethical least of all against the residents of what we now understand as the Global South. The political subjects that concern Malcolm X are tasked with carving out a space of political existence *within* the established political order. I said above that this quasi-spatial understanding of political space on the part of Malcolm X sets itself up as "new." That idea needs qualification.

George Lipsitz's text, *How Racism Takes Place*, and his conceptualization of spatial imaginaries, is useful here. Lipsitz proposes that racism is dependent upon the existence of racial imaginaries that are spaces of exclusion.

The white spatial imaginary has cultural as well as social consequences. It structures feelings as well as social institutions. The white spatial imaginary idealizes "pure" and homogenous spaces, controlled environments, and predictable patterns of design and behavior … Among dominant groups in the United States, socially shared moral geographies have long infused places with implicit ethical assumptions about the proper forms of social connection and separation. Historian David W. Noble identifies a spatial imaginary at the heart of European conquest and settlement of North America in the seventeenth century. Republican theorists in the Renaissance juxtaposed virtuous and timeless nature with corrupt and time-bound human society. They believed that free nations had to be composed of homogenous populations with ties to the national landscape, to "timeless spaces" where citizens lived in complete harmony with one another. Starting in the seventeenth century, European settler colonialists imagined that American space might offer a refuge from the corruptions of European time. Coalescing around what Noble calls "the metaphor of two worlds" – the idea of America as an island of virtue in a global sea of corruption – these ideals became institutionalized within the national culture of the United States through the writings of transcendentalists, the visual art of the Hudson River School, evocations by historians of the frontier as a unique source of regeneration, and ultimately, in the ideal of the private properly ordered suburban home and homogenous community.

Yet in order to have pure and homogenous spaces, "impure" populations have to be removed and marginalized.[2]

I would like to extend Lipsitz's argument in service of establishing a framework for understanding the logic of Malcolm X's political philosophy with respect to geography. What I mean here is that all political projects are, at their foundation, imaginary. This is exemplified by the concept of Manifest Destiny that speaks to the project of land theft and genocide that establishes the geographic spatiality of the United States of America as one clear example. The idea of the United States as a white nation that extends from "sea to shining sea" that is ordained by a higher power is, at its outset, an imagined spatiality that finds a "real" space in which to fulfill its logic. There is no clear separation between the intellectual process illuminated by Lipsitz as the font of racism, political projects informed by imagined ideal spaces, and that presented in the political philosophy of Malcolm X to unravel the marginalization of Black people. Both require the foundation of the practical political project to be something imagined. The alteration expresses itself in the manner in which "imagined" spatiality becomes "real."

A useful way of considering this framework is to think of the notion of imagined and real spatiality as a Venn diagram. The first image would appear with the known world as a clearly demarcated circle with the imagination of new worlds as less distinct and non-overlapping orbs. The first of these represents the white spatial imaginary prior to 1492 and the "discovery" of the New World. The white spatial imaginary is demarcated by the limited geography of the landmass of Europe that explains the centuries of conflict and the desire for exploration. The imaginary, in this temporal context, operates at the level of mythology that is represented by the "state of nature" in the thinking of Hobbes that presupposes an indistinct and fictional existence. The legend of Prester John is an exemplar of this logic and the problematic represented by the limitation of geography in the white spatial imaginary at the time.

With the discovery of the New World, the white spatial imaginary begins to shape the indistinct geographic space of the newly "discovered" Americas with myths that reify and extend their own political, theological and existential understanding of the world that essentializes the nature of indigenous people as Noble Savages and the African people as savages. The formerly indistinct orb would begin to take shape and also start to overlap with the reality-based geography of the European world that has now begun to extend its influence.

The next stage in this thinking is the evolution of the white spatial imaginary driven by the seemingly limitless space of the Americas that concretizes itself as Manifest Destiny. The 1872 painting, *American Progress*, by John Gast, is an exemplar of this logic (see Figure 8).

Figure 8   American Progress, by John Gast (1872)

The painting is dominated by the colossal presence of "Columbia," the idealized white female figure who here is floating across the landscape, stringing telegraph line behind her, while indigenous people and animals flee. White settlers march alongside Columbia's progress and illustrate various levels of technological advancement from the most basic mode of locomotion (on horseback and foot) to that of the railroad. Perhaps iron-ically, the book that Columbia wields is not the Bible or the Constitution but a text labeled simply "School Book." The presumption here, in the absence of any explicit representation of coercive threat, is that it is the superior intellect of white people that propels them to fulfill the promise of Manifest Destiny. Technology and its implication for the employment of force are secondary or even tertiary to the informed wisdom of this endeavor. The way to visualize this phenomenon is to imagine that the prospect of the white spatial imaginary exceeds the boundaries of the indistinct geographic spatiality available to the settlers. This is an important intellectual return to the state of thinking prior to 1492, when the white spatial imaginary exceeded the available space and also conflicted with the political projects of others in the same geographic spatiality. Here, the existence of indigenous peoples who have their own political imaginary and geographic spatiality for its fulfillment explicates the conflicts and genocidal project of the white settlers. Further, there is diabolical logic exemplified by the Missouri Compromise of 1820, and its repeal by the Kansas–Nebraska Act of 1854, that sought to clarify the role of slavery and the Black people who suffered under its logic as the project of geographic expansion of the idealized white political space marched west. The final visualization renders the formerly imagined and indistinct spatiality of Manifest Destiny as indistinguishable from the real geographic space of the United States of America. The phantasm has become real.

What is left to consider in the aftermath of this political evolution is the existence of political subjects that fracture the imperative exposed by Lipsitz of "pure and homogenous spaces." This becomes particularly complex in the aftermath of the Civil War and the ratification of the Thirteenth, Fourteenth and Fifteenth Amendments. These amendments render inoperative the logic of Article 1 of the Constitution and the apportionment of the original distribution of legislative power (*logos*) as a product of the sub-human nature of people of African descent who were understood to be three-fifths human in Madison's Federalist 54 and its Compromise. This requires the establishment of abstract zones of exception that become realized political spaces in the appearance of reservations, ghettos and prisons that are internal to the imaginary, become real, but exist as distinguishable from the way of being of the "host" entity.

In the case of the notion of Manifest Destiny, the circle that represents the ideology completely overlaps the available geographic spatiality. The spatial imaginary becomes a reality with all of the political implications of that phenomenon in the case of the white supremacist political project that establishes the Negro. Lipsitz proposes the following with respect to the black spatial imaginary under these conditions.

Black people pay an enormous price for the coupling of race and place that permeate society. Pervasive racial segregation creates a geographically organized vulnerability for Blacks. Not only are they concentrated demographically, but the processes that turn white privilege and power into the accumulation of assets that appreciate in value and can be passed down across generations, also leave Black people with little control over the economic decisions that shape their lives. Discriminatory lending and investment practices mean that outsiders own most of the businesses in Black communities. As Malcolm X used to rhyme, "when the sun goes down, our money goes to another part of town."[3]

There is a way in which reflecting on the process of marginalization based upon race that reveals itself most prominently in the form of segregated spaces where access to capital in the form of housing as an asset and the operation of business enterprises tends toward a Marxist reading of this phenomenon that perhaps overdetermines the role of capital. In other words, it proves useful to understand capital and its possession, movement, etc., as the most obvious manifestation of systems of marginalization but it must be carefully examined to ensure the correct demarcation of cause from effect. The argument that I am promoting here is that Malcolm X employs the obvious disparity in economic power between the white and Black communities as the manner in which he establishes the intellectual buy-in by his audience. This does not mean that the economic argument is not important, but rather seeks to position it, correctly, as the effect of a particular cause. This is clear in the 1964 speech known as "The Ballot or the Bullet," where Malcolm X proposes the following ordering principle with respect to political or economic viability.

> By ballot I only mean freedom. Don't you know – I disagree with Lomax on this issue – that the ballot is more important than the dollar? Can I prove it? Yes. Look in the UN. There are poor nations in the UN; yet those poor nations can get together with their voting power and keep the rich nations from making a move ... So, the ballot is more important.[4]

What Malcolm X is proposing is first recognition of this condition that is addressed by a project that imagines its reversal through a process of self-realization *in situ* that ends up in freedom that can be understood as productively related to the freedom represented by the ballot. Recall this passage quoted in the Introduction:

> This is the type of philosophy that we want to express among our people. We don't need to give them a program, not yet. First, give them something to think about. If we give them something to think about and start them thinking in a way that they should think, they'll see through all this camouflage that's going on right now. It's just a show – the result of a script written for somebody else. The people will take that script and tear it up and write one for themselves. And you can bet that when you write the script for yourself, you're always doing something different than you'd be doing if you followed somebody else's script.[5]

Here, Malcolm X seems to be proposing a form of racial imaginary that is discernible, through the thinking of Lipsitz, as the recognition of the condition of subjugation followed by a project that imagines a different subjectivity. This is critically related to the practice of segregation creating what I have referred to here as "zones of exception" within the totalizing context of the racial imaginary that finds itself expressed as "real" geographic spatiality. It is important here to understand Malcolm X's complex understanding of segregation as a concept and its relationship to something like separation or independence within an established societal order. He elaborates this in "The Ballot or the Bullet."

> Let me explain what I mean. A segregated district or community is a community in which people live, but outsiders control the politics and the economy of that community. They never refer to the white section as a segregated community. It's the all-Negro section that's a segregated community. Why? The white man controls his own school, his own bank, his own economy, his own politics, his own everything, his own community – but he also controls yours. When you're under someone else's control you're segregated. They'll always give you the lowest or the worst that there is to offer, but it doesn't mean you're segregated just because you have your own. You've got to control your own. Just like the white man has control of his, you need control of yours.[6]

Explaining this framework, one can understand the nature of the white supremacist project of Manifest Destiny as requiring the existence of spaces of segregation that affirm the power dynamic and sovereignty of the state as formed. This notion of segregation and the vector of power is manifest in the previous chapter's exploration of police power in the form of brutality that is employed by the state to create the space for the existence and, at the same time, marginalization, of the "so-called Negro." There is a way in which this understanding dys-forms, while at the same time leans upon, the logic of biopower developed by Michel Foucault. Foucault understands power as existing in the episteme that concerns him and overlaps that of the modern (Black) Atlantic as a manifestation of a form of power that is so omnipresent that it recedes from observation in its obscurity through its ubiquity. There are additional elements of Foucault's thought that facilitate a more complete understanding of the elements of Malcolm X's philosophical system that deal with the apparatus of government considered by the French philosopher.

What proves interesting here is Foucault's formulation of biopower, which he unpacks in some detail in the lectures from 1977 and 1978, published as *Security, Territory, Population: Lectures at the Collège de France 1977–1978*, that turn upon his understanding of the penal force of the state in a similar manner to the thinking of Malcolm X and his preoccupation with police brutality. Foucault elaborates a tripartite relationship to security that, when juxtaposed to Malcolm X's understanding of the societal relationship to the minuet of duties and rights for the "so-called Negro," is inoperative. What Foucault proposes is that "security" as such is a product of "laying down a law and fixing a punishment for the person who breaks it."[7] Recall that Malcolm X identifies that the "so-called Negro," in their coercion by police power in the absence of a violation of law, therefore, fundamentally begins this subjective relationship with security in a distinct yet related manner than that of the normative subject that functions within what Foucault calls the "legal or juridical mechanism."

The second of these "mechanisms" is explicated in Foucault's January 14, 1978 lecture:

I will now return to the second mechanism, the law framed by mechanisms of surveillance and correction, which is, of course, the disciplinary mechanism. The disciplinary mechanism is characterized by the fact that a third personage, the culprit, appears within the binary system of the code, and at the same time, outside the code, and outside the legislative act that establishes the law and the juridical act that punishes the culprit, a series of adjacent, detective, medical, and psychological techniques appear which fall within the domain of surveillance, diagnosis, and the possible transformation of individuals.[8]

What Malcolm X illustrates here is that the "so-called Negro" is always already the "culprit" in the parlance of Foucault, and in this relationship of outsider in the absence of process or violation, the logic explicated in *Security, Territory, Population* is reversed. The subject is immediately transformed from human to Negro because of the fracturing of the logic of the first mechanism and therefore it follows that these subjects are preternaturally subject to the surveillance described here. The third mechanism proposed by Foucault:

> … is based on the same matrix, with the same penal law, the same punishments, and the same type of framework of surveillance on one side and correction on the other, but now, the application of this penal law, the development of preventative measures, and the organization of corrective punishments will be governed by the following kind of questions. For example: What is the average rate of criminality for this [type]? How can we predict statistically the number of thefts at a given moment, in a given society, in a given town, in the town or in the country, in a given social stratum, and so on?[9]

This is at odds with the understanding developed by Malcolm X of both police power and ultimately segregation as a product of its kinetic employment. The philosophical system of Malcolm X necessarily diverges from that of Foucault, which presupposes a form of existence that is based upon universal proportional marginalization of political subjects *vis-à-vis* the state as a product of citizenship. Foucault's notion of power that radiates from the state and envelops the polity in universal fashion is at a distance from a form of power that disproportionately affects or dys-forms subjects. Malcolm X perceives the phenomenon of state power as force instead. Here I am interested in parsing an understanding of violence as a *force* in a particular manner. This is in contradistinction to Foucault's employment of "Power" to represent the phenomenon of governmentality in the form of oppression. I am proposing here that we recall that "Power" is a measure of "Force." This project is concerned with "the thing itself" not only in its measure but also its directionality. Employing the term "Power" does not facilitate that analysis. The definition employed in physics reveals the limitation: "In physics, power is the rate of doing work. It is the amount of energy consumed per unit time. Having no direction, it is a scalar quantity."[10] Force, on the other hand has the following definition: "In physics, a force is any interaction that, when unopposed, will change the motion of an object. In other words, a force can cause an object with mass to change its velocity (which includes to begin moving from a state of rest), i.e., to accelerate. Force can also be described by intuitive concepts such as a push or a pull. A force has both magnitude and direction, making it a vector quantity."[11] It is the vector quality of the force of police violence that becomes the engine of segregation that establishes this exceptional space.

Moving forward armed with the thinking of Lipsitz, Foucault and Malcolm X, the framing of the imperative of real geographic space becomes a possibility for forms of subjective recreation though not an imperative. Meaning that by altering the condition of force as manifesting segregation there is a possibility for the Black imaginary to exist as a space *within* an existing and/or competing imaginary; ideologically or spatially. Garveyism typifies this logic.

In the absence of a practical strategy for the occupation of a specific geographic space without the negative ethical implications of projects of conquest and colonialism, Malcolm X imagines a form of political existence that accommodates the white and Black political imaginaries within the established geographic space available.

Elements of E. J. Hobsbawm's canonical *Nations and Nationalism since 1780: Programme, Myth, Reality* are useful here as we approach the deconstruction of Malcolm X's understanding of Black Nationalism and its relationship to a particular form of "international relation-ism" amongst marginalized political subjects. Hobsbawm describes the imperative of understanding the differentiation between the nation and nationalism and most importantly the intellectual peril of rendering these definitions static. He writes the following, indulgently quoted here for its importance to framing this thinking:

While this has, especially since the 1960s, led to some attempts at nation-building by consciousness-raising, it is not a legitimate criticism of observers as sophisticated as Otto Bauer and Renan, who knew perfectly well that nations also had objective elements in common. Nevertheless, to insist on consciousness or choice as the criterion of nationhood is insensibly to subordinate the complex and multiple ways in which human beings define and redefine themselves as members of groups, to a single option: the choice of belonging to a "nation" or "nationality". Politically or administratively such a choice must today be made by virtue of living in states which supply passports or ask questions about language in censuses. Yet even today it is perfectly possible for a person living in Slough to think of himself, depending on circumstances, as – say – a British citizen, or (faced with other citizens of a different colour) as an Indian, or (faced with other Indians) as a Gujarati, or (faced with Hindus or Muslims) as a Jain, or as a member of a particular caste, or kinship connection, or as one who, at home, speaks Hindi rather than Gujarati, or doubtless in other ways. Nor indeed is it possible to reduce even "nationality" to a single dimension, whether political, cultural or otherwise (unless, of course, obliged to do so by *force majeure* of states). People can identify themselves as Jews even though they share neither religion, language, culture, tradition, historical background, blood-group patterns nor an attitude to the Jewish state. Nor does this imply a purely subjective definition of "the nation".

Neither objective nor subjective definitions are thus satisfactory, and both are misleading. In any case, agnosticism is the best initial posture of a student in this field, and so this book assumes no *a priori* definition of what constitutes a nation. As an initial working definition [is that] any sufficiently large body of people whose members regard themselves as members of a "nation", will be treated as such.[12]

There is much to unpack here in that the thought of Malcolm X is inextricable from any intellectual genealogy of Black Nationalism. Further, the fact of the need for something like "Black Nationalism" is a direct result of the evolution of the nation and nationalism traced by Hobsbawm that finds its ultimate expression in the formation of "new" nations in the "new" world. The first point of tension between this excerpt from Hobsbawm and the thinking of Malcolm X is what can be understood as the author's concern with "consciousness" representing the *sine qua non* of national identity or robust belonging to a nation. The simple answer here is that the operative term in the thinking of Hobsbawm is "human" that leads him to assert the multiple ways in which human beings are capable of asserting themselves and forming relations that can be characterized as nations. This, for Hobsbawm, means that "consciousness" has nothing to do with a claim on humanity but rather a claim on membership in a social collective. For Malcolm X, the discourse of the Negro renders consciousness and recognition of humanity as the threshold conditions for a project of national identity or subjective belonging. What this means for Malcolm X is that the national formation that preoccupies him and serves as the bridge to other, more traditional forms of state formation, if not the end in and of itself, is a consciousness of *human-ness* that is recognizable by other social formations in the same way that nation-states are privileged and recognized. Therefore, recognized membership in the community of humanity rather than being understood through the exclusionary status of "Negro" (a subject that is substantively sub-human as well as marginally eligible for citizenship) becomes, for Malcolm X, a type of national identity. What this means in praxis is that the personal and sovereign space of the formerly excluded Negro becomes a *mobile* form of political possibility that is free to associate itself with other subjects or political formations at will. With respect to domestic political life, examination calls for revisiting Malcolm X's conceptualization of segregation that speaks to the vector of power relations. This logic is foundational to understanding how Black Separatism operates within the established political space of the United States of America.

As a practical matter, this phenomenon is not far removed from our understanding of revolutionary forms of existence found in the maroon communities in the Atlantic World during the eighteenth and nineteenth centuries. A quick examination of the terms and conditions of maroon society in a place like Jamaica is instructive. The fact of Jamaican maroon society was not a project for the formation of an independent state but quasi-autonomy within the co-located borders of British colonial/slave society; maroon society. Malcolm X engages in what productively might be framed as an informed reading of Sherman's Field Order 15, which must be expanded beyond its well-known tag-line "40 acres and a mule." In my reading, the field order is better read as a gesture toward the type of sovereign existence within an existing set of national boundaries that is proposed by Malcolm X's understanding of the force relations most easily recognized in segregated communities. Sherman's order is instructive here in that it provides an intellectual bridge to understanding the elements of international relations theory that I argue represent a useful way of examining this philosophical system. Sherman's order proposed the following:

SPECIAL FIELD ORDERS, No. 15.
I. The islands from Charleston, south, the abandoned rice fields along the rivers for thirty miles back from the sea, and the country bordering the St. Johns river, Florida, are reserved and set apart for the settlement of the negroes now made free by the acts of war and the proclamation of the President of the United States.

Here we witness the imperative of geography imposed by two important limitations: the limited amount of land available, which is understood to be the sovereign possession of the United States of America. Here, Sherman, through the exceptional power of the state that exists during time of conflict, carves out a defined space that is further understood to exist in the following manner:

II. At Beaufort, Hilton Head, Savannah, Fernandina, St. Augustine and Jacksonville, the blacks may remain in their chosen or accustomed vocations – but on the islands, and in the settlements hereafter to be established, *no white person whatever, unless military officers and soldiers detailed for duty, will be permitted to reside* [my italics]; and the sole and exclusive management of affairs will be left to the freed people themselves, subject only to the United States military authority and the acts of Congress. By the laws of war, and orders of the President of the United States, the negro is free and must be dealt with as such. He cannot be subjected to conscription or forced military service, save by the written orders of the highest military authority of the Department, under such regulations as the President or Congress may prescribe. Domestic servants, blacksmiths, carpenters and other mechanics, will be free to select their own work and residence, but the young and able-bodied negroes must be encouraged to enlist as soldiers in the service of the United States, to contribute their share towards maintaining their own freedom, and securing their rights as citizens of the United States.[13]

The fracturing of the power/force dynamic of segregation as forced separation is important to examine here. If we begin with Malcolm X's assertion that "[a] segregated district or community is a community in which people live, but outsiders control the politics and the economy of that community," what Sherman appears to be proposing is that the internal operation of this territory be controlled by the resident freed-persons but includes a recognition of the imperative of force to support and defend that status. His order disallows the presence of whites unless detailed as members of the garrison to support the boundaries of this territory. Cynically, or perhaps logically, this can be seen as both a deterrent to prevent the expansion or development of military force to challenge the sovereignty of the United States but it also alters this power dynamic from what Malcolm X understands as segregation to *marronage*.

Harlem, as a profoundly segregated space that suffers from the dual arms of marginalization – the coercive power of the state exhibited by police brutality and economic extraction (colonialism) – in the parlance of Malcolm X, in the absence of the possibility of a sovereign nation-state, can, through the amelioration of these conditions, achieve a status similar to that proposed by Field Order 15 or exhibited in the maroon societies of the eighteenth and nineteenth centuries. What this means is that the embodied personal consciousness-driven subjectivity of the Black body finds a geographic space in which to reside and form relations with others through an exhibition of sovereign will. Hegel is relevant here and Malcolm's preoccupation with his thinking is well founded. Marable noted his interest in this philosopher's work, writing:

Sometimes Malcolm would be deeply engrossed in reading some book very obscure to Thomas. One author he vividly recalled was philosopher G. W. F. Hegel. "Hegel was his man," Thomas recalled, possibly referring to the same passages on "lordship and bondage" that had also fascinated Frantz Fanon.[14]

Further study by Malcolm X of Hegel's body of work would have revealed a common understanding in the *Philosophy of Right*,[15] where the German asserts that the family is "completed in three stages":

a) Marriage, the form assumed by the concept of the family in its immediate stage;

b) Family Property and Capital (the external embodiment of the concept) and;

c) The Education of Children and the Dissolution of the Family.

Within the separate communities proposed by Malcolm X, the individual sovereign subject is free to form the associations of the family that include economic control and education that allow for the formation of something like the "state." This is where the thinking of Malcolm X takes a quantum leap forward and establishes a system of international community that informs what I have presented as the possibility of understanding this form of political existence as quasi-territorial and internationally recognized.

International recognition (specifically) and recognition (generally) are thick concepts that are a product of Malcolm X's physical and metaphysical journey beyond the boundaries of the United States. This motion served, perhaps paradoxically, to reaffirm his subjective existence as dependent upon the United States while at the same time outside of it, through a series of contextual relations based upon an internationally-recognized status, as being an aggrieved victim of white supremacy in the form of colonialism and empire. This is explicit in excerpts from his speech from April 8, 1964, known as "The Black Revolution."

> The greatest weapon the colonial powers have used in the past against the people has always been divide-and-conquer. America is a colonial power. She has colonized 22 million Afro-Americans by depriving us of first-class citizenship, by depriving us of civil rights, actually by depriving us of human rights. She has not only deprived us of the right to be a citizen, she has deprived us of the right to be human beings, the right to be recognized and respected as men and women. In this country the black can be fifty years old and he is still a "boy."[16]

Malcolm X understands this colonialism not only as a system of internal division of the Black community in the United States, asserting his awareness of how America "...plays one Negro leader against the other,"[17] but also as a continuation of the logic of the erasure of the Middle Passage which caused the separation of American Blacks from the rest of the world that begins to find resolution in his system of thought through consciousness of a common oppressive logic. The text of "The Ballot or the Bullet" emphasizes his thinking on this point:

> Whereas the other segment or section in America, known as black nationalists, are more interested in human rights than they are in civil rights. And they place more stress on human rights than they do on

civil rights. The difference between the thinking and the scope of the Negroes who are involved in the human-rights struggle and those "So-Called" Negroes involved in the human-rights struggle don't look upon themselves as Americans ...

So in this country you find two different types of Afro-Americans – the type who looks upon himself as a minority and you as the majority, because his scope is limited to the American scene; and then you have the type who looks upon himself as part of a majority and you as part of a microscopic minority.[18]

What proves definitive for Malcolm X here is the intellectual shift with respect to his political ambition from the largely domestic concern of civil rights to the fundamental and transnational consideration of human rights. This resonates with the argument traced through Hobsbawm's concern with respect to what he understands to be the reduction of national belonging to fundamental consciousness. What Malcolm X is asserting is that the first right of all human kind is to be recognized as human; from that position, political projects of various types might proceed. Further, he asserts that the common experience of the denial of human status generally, through cultural, economic, political and social oppression, creates subjects in common for whom an identity can be forged. Thinking and saying this is one matter, but finding the apparatus in the established world system for this ideology proved frustrating. Manning Marable's text documents Malcolm X's frustration with being unable to achieve support from the African continent for his initiative to link racism in the United States to white supremacy in the form of colonialism and empire on the African continent. Marable writes:

In the end, Malcolm failed to persuade, though not for any great flaw in his argument or ebbing of his passion; his rhetoric simply could not overcome the cold logic of international politics. In the bipolar political world of the 1960s, backing a formal resolution that sharply condemned the United States for its domestic human rights violations would have been seen by the American governments as an act of partnership with the Soviet Union or the communist Chinese.[19]

Marable's reading of this situation is true in some measure but can be enhanced by taking stock of the internal logic of nationalism that was sweeping the African continent at the time. This problem, in many ways, speaks to the circularity of logic that Malcolm X recognizes and centers as the preoccupation of his political philosophy: membership in a nation or a sense of nationalism is not just independent of recognizable geographic borders but necessary for certain subjects to work against the struggles for national independence that were sweeping the African continent at the time. The threshold issue that confounds the political ambition of Malcolm X, recalling the argument in the earlier chapter on ontology, is once again displacement. The total erasure of something like a legacy of belonging to a recognized political space in the nationalist political context creates the necessity for an alternative political project while, at the same time, confounding that effort. From the perspective of the leaders of newly independent African nations, not only do they have *realpolitik* to consider with respect to the potential for retribution by the United States government but also confusion in the logic of their own movements that are a product of a consciousness of belonging based upon geographic spatiality and culture. Both of these elements of national identity-making are oppositional to the reality of the diasporic African–American struggling to leave behind the status of Negro. The effort to develop a nationalist political project based upon extra-territorial and extra-national belonging requires attention. If we understand that Malcolm X is fundamentally interested in the notion of culture, we can understand that in a multivalent fashion he recognizes oppression (here framed as colonialism) as creating a particular form of political subject. That political subject, formed through coercive force, exists in a space that necessitates amelioration of that circumstance. That necessity calls for a form of collective activity that forms systems of political belonging that are based on the collective experience of white supremacy, not only as an organizing principle surrounding the notion of independence, but also with respect to belonging. This becomes a practical political problem for the territorial imperative explicit in the primordial argument for self-governance that was lifted from Woodrow Wilson and his notion of self-determination.

The central tenets of Wilsonian nationalism, presented on May 27, 1916, "called for the establishment of a mechanism for international cooperation among sovereign states based upon two related principles: one was that political arrangements ... should be based on ... the consent of the governed." The second was that "all political arrangements of consent should relate to one another as equals."[20] The fact that Wilson never intended or considered that political actors outside of the

European context might take his statements to heart did not encumber the portability of these ideas. The specific context here is the adoption of the "language of self-determination ... by groups that made claims directed at victorious powers, either to demand political independence, as in Ireland, or to ask for recognition of rights within an existing polity, as with leading African–American activists like W. E. B. Du Bois and Wilson Monroe Trotter."[21] It is important to explore this intellectual genealogy in order to ensure we account for the influence of Negritude with respect to nationalist movements in Africa and how Malcolm X absorbs and improvises in and around its logic.

The influence of Du Bois and the Harlem Renaissance on the roots of Negritude had been identified as early as the 1920s. The language adopted by the Negritude movement is apparent in a "1922 issue of *The Crisis* magazine [where] Du Bois suggests that not only are whites and other persons in power denying the achievements of African people, but that African people also aided whites by neglecting the abilities and achievements of their African peers."[22] Leopold Senghor's thinking is useful in developing the analysis regarding the complexity of Malcolm X's brand of internationalism framed as a particular strain of Pan-African thinking. Defining Pan-Africanism and Negritude is essential to pushing along this logical continuum. Abiola Irele offers the following in the 1965 issue of *The Journal of Modern African Studies*.

> Pan-Africanism has been described as essentially a movement of "emotion and ideas," and this description is equally applicable to negritude, which is its cultural parallel. Indeed, no better phrase could be found to sum up its double nature, first as a psychological response to the social and cultural conditions of the "colonial situation" and secondly as a quest for a new and original orientation ... Negritude is thus at the same time a literary and ideological movement.[23]

Senghor's praxis as a political actor as well as cultural icon and artist found its expression in his concept of African socialism; essentially, Negritude's answer to the modern nation-state. "Senghor's concept of negritude antedates his formal concern with African Socialism, but is connected with it intimately through its early militant emphasis on the primacy of Africa and later African cultural values."[24] Rather than diverting the attention of this text to Senghor, it is useful to follow the methodological logic here that situates Malcolm X as intellectually related to Du Bois and Fanon and in that vein briefly examine the latter's careful engagement with Negritude in *Black Skin, White Masks*.

Fanon draws this intellectual construct into his narrative, interrogating Senghor's *Ce que l'homme noir apporte*.

> That is how tyranny of rhythm affects what is least intellectual in us, allowing us to penetrate the spirituality of the object; and that lack of constraint which is ours is itself rhythmic. [Senghor] "Have I [Fanon's narrator] read it correctly? I give it an even closer reading. On the other side of the white world there lies a magnificent black culture. Negro sculpture! I begin to blush with pride. Was this our salvation?"[25]

Here Fanon proposes a geography for this worldview with one of two possible interpretations. The world is white and on the far side of it, hidden, lies Black culture, or; the white world and Black culture live together in a unified space and Fanon, from his vantage point, is denied access to Black culture by the imposition of the white world. Either case poses a significant challenge. One must either journey to Black culture across the expanse of the white world or surmount the obstruction only to be presented with a further challenge. Can Black culture morph into a "world" to compete with, coexist or replace the white world that is empirically present? The fact of Fanon's narrator "blush[ing] with pride" demonstrates the wit with which the author confronts these threats to his very existence.

Senghor's political ideology proposes a solution. "[Senghor's] African Socialism is a flexible doctrine in gestation, adapted to the African context, designed to facilitate the transition to modernization and to project a vision of a better future. It is a part of African nationalism. As such, it is not the arrogant universalistic nationalism of race pretending to offer the just and only basis for the future. It proclaims the equality, rather than the superiority of Africa."[26] This equality is measured against the implicit understanding that the nation-state, as articulated in the Western political tradition and defined by Wilsonian nationalism, is the highest form of social order. African socialism therefore privileged this analysis and elaborated an improvisation on the theme that allowed for the combination of the universe of African states to work in cooperation and counterpoint to the European/American model, just as Negritude elaborates African content within the existing European political structure: more specifically, African content articulated in French through the lens of the European surrealist literary tradition.

The "problem" with Negritude is visible in the debate between Fanon and Sartre that proposes that Negritude is dedicated to its own destruction; it is transition and not result, a means and not the ultimate goal. The final stage, something like the creation and maintenance of a post-colonial world, eludes Fanon; the thought of Malcolm X, in its radical progressivism, seeks to resolve this tension.

Malcolm X seems to propose, from the manifold exposition of a system of existential philosophy that establishes identity from a position of erasure (in the same sense that Negritude employs "mythology"), a solution to the problem that confounds the thinking of Fanon in *Black Skin, White Masks*. What Malcolm X presents is the notion that the shared experience of coercion that creates the necessity of mythmaking for the diasporic figure as well as the primordial figure in Africa renders the possibility of a post-colonial existence that renders geographic location and discernible borders useful in establishing the existence of African states in the world community, but not a requirement for membership in that state.

Perhaps a way to envisage this extension of the thinking of Fanon and its relationship to tracing the ideas that Malcolm X is engaged in unraveling is to return to *marronage* as the theme around which he improvises. Maroons existed in a state of marginalized sovereignty in that the bodies of subjects of the maroon state were only recognized as protected by the "state" to the extent that they remained within the borders established through the agreement of the colonial state and the Other. This state of being can be productively understood as substantively similar to the way Malcolm X understands segregation as a negative formation that privileges the radical power differential between the segregator and segregated, whereby the vector of force is recognizable in its expression toward the marginalized subject. The logic of *marronage* disperses this force vector without imploding it. This is exemplified by the limitation of the status of sovereign self only within borders that are substantively defined by the same logic of coercion. Malcolm X is proposing a complex understanding of the separation as an exemplar of willfulness and further the maintenance of the body as a sovereign space in its relationship to this brand of national identity within the borders of a nation-state or without. This concept only seems irrational because it has to do with Black bodies and their perception as always unstable with respect to freedom and recognition because of the coercive, subject dys-forming nature of white supremacy.

Recall the argument that Malcolm X views the body as a political space that has the same accoutrements as the geographic political space of the state as a corrective to the systematic erasure of the possibility of belonging. There is a way in which the idea of the metaphysical rescue of the Black body from the marginalization of being a Negro is a radical reconstruction of the terms and conditions of political subjectivity. The goal here for Malcolm X is to establish a metaphysical recovery of Black identity that then (similar to the employment of Manifest Destiny) serves as the engine for a coherent and recognizable political project. The complication is evident in the fact that the restoration of Black sovereign political subjectivity does not necessarily presuppose a wholesale alteration of the terms and conditions of white supremacist logic. This assembles a problem for this system of thinking that expresses itself in the following fashion:

1. Malcolm X's "so-called Negro" is a wholly political being whose existence has no political relevance except its irrelevance;
2. The Black subject implodes this by taking on a newly-formed persona to elide this political irrelevance;
3. This new self-referentially relevant political figure is in search of recognition for its political identity that is not forthcoming from the current political context or world system;
4. In order to resolve this, the subject in question seeks political recognition on its own terms, reversing the normative political understanding of the subject being defined by the state;
5. This subject defines its own political self and can then choose its association and present the basis for its recognition as a shared experience of coercion;
6. The body becomes its own passport that allows it to choose its political associations.

This body then is analogous to the settlements proposed by Sherman's Field Order that find themselves in a position of needing technology for the protection of that identity. One such "technology" is Islam as a way of being that is necessarily transnational in ways that are similar to Malcolm X's most evolved understanding of this form of political subjectivity.

I have backgrounded the influence of Islam in the philosophical system of Malcolm X for reasons that revolve around his own assertion that he would not allow his faith to prevent the formation of alliances that he found essential to fulfilling his political project. However, there are elements of Islam that I believe model for Malcolm X the manner in which he would imagine his new political being. I'm specifically interested in three elements of the faith: (1) its orientation away from the West; (2) its performative nature; and (3) its alternative temporality.

The necessity that practitioners of Islam orient their bodies and minds toward Mecca requires them to frame their existence in transnational terms in the same manner I have argued that the resolved Black Nationalist must in this system. It is important to note that their point of focus does not erase the current spatiality of the subject because in order to know the direction of "There" one must be sure of the "Here." Explicit in this orientation toward Mecca is the fact that it has to be "performed" in order for the subject to fulfill the requirements of being a Muslim. You cannot *be* a non-compliant Muslim. In the same way that Malcolm's system here requires a "practice" of refuting the imperatives of white supremacy at every turn, as exemplified by his unwavering commitment to the abandonment of his "slave name," the practitioner of Islam must be just that: practicing. The commitment to the practice that requires this dis(re)orientation five times a day frames the final element of Islam that preoccupies me here: the establishment of an alternative temporal regime that is understood most properly as political and subject-forming and maintaining.

The temporality of Islam, and here I'm thinking of the daily requirement of Salat and the annual period of Ramadan and the way in which they overcome the secular temporality of any system of governance. It additionally allows the subject to explicitly "check out" of the common flow of societal order in the same way that the diasporic "so-called Negro" must be distant while at the same time fully aware of the historical terms of their subjective marginalization. This form of radical rejection and reestablishment of the terms of ontological being, corporeal existence and spatiality necessarily leads to Malcolm X's philosophy of revolution.

4

Revolution

Malcolm X, like Frantz Fanon, struggles to find the proper mechanism(s) to employ to rescue the formerly marginalized subject first from their depraved self-hatred, then to find a space of recognition for that refashioned subject and finally the means of preserving that place of peace. What Malcolm X is perhaps reductively most famously known for is the exhortation "By Any Means Necessary," which implies that those means include, and in fact privilege, violence as the means to the end of political viability. Fanon's opening chapter in *The Wretched of the Earth*, "Concerning Violence," has generally overwhelmed his system of thought in the same manner that this exhortation has the thought of Malcolm X, rendering these thinkers the biblical father and son to the holy ghost of violence that would become the Black Panther Party and the African National Congress in the eyes of some beholders. In neither case is violence *not* part of the story, but in neither case is violence *all* of the story.

Throughout this text I have had to resort to proposing that many of the elements of the previous chapters, on ontology, the body and geographic space, would find themselves resolved in the discussion surrounding the question of "revolution." This is substantively because all roads lead to the dual necessities of law-establishing or law-maintaining conflict, in the sense that Walter Benjamin understands violence. This was discussed in some depth in the chapter on the body and its relationship to police brutality. Malcolm X understands violence as useful and in large measure imperative in at least two ways. First, as a tool for extracting the body from the harmful quagmire of coerced political subjectivity. Second as a means either to alter the totality of a political context or in service of the protection of spatiality or the realization of a recognition of a sovereign political project that is protected against coercive encroachment. The aim of this chapter is to unpack Malcolm X's philosophy of revolution or, more appropriately, to identify how revolution fits into his philosophical system, which may, in the end, be most appropriately identified as itself a philosophy of revolution. The focus will generally be on two essential speeches from April 1964, "The Ballot or the Bullet" and "The Black Revolution," which will be read together as a coherent single statement and framed against the philosophical thinking applied to resolving issues of ontology, the body and geographic space. Structurally what this implies is that the discourse of revolution is both the ultimate resolution to the logic of the system and the fuel which propels it forward.

I have proposed that the two speeches from April 3 ("The Ballot or the Bullet") and April 8 ("The Black Revolution") be read as a coherent single statement. First, much of the latter is a recasting of the essential elements of the former, but the opening moments of "The Black Revolution" serve as the resolution to the tension established by the implications of "The Ballot or the Bullet." That tension, simply stated, is to evaluate the most effective means of securing rights for African–Americans between the discourse of civil versus human rights. What I mean to propose is that Malcolm X, in parsing civil versus human rights, is reifying the notion I illuminated in the previous chapter that the political reality of Black (American) being is transnational in its unstable presence in any defined political space. This raises, in the thinking of Malcolm X, a juridical problem for employing civil rights as the means to ameliorate this condition.

In unpacking this, it is apparent that Malcolm X witnesses democracy, as practiced in the United States specifically, as morally bankrupt in that it is dedicated to the marginalization of certain political subjects as fuel for white supremacy. He is explicit in this claim in "The Black Revolution" where he frames "white nationalism [as what] ... you call democracy."[1] It is in the April 3 speech that he makes the case against the US government's institutions as sufficient for addressing the problem that it has (actively) caused the deprivation of Black people and in doing so is morally bankrupt. This thinking is predicated on his argument that the Black body is excluded from the logic of democracy in that the laws as such are not applicable and have to be further clarified to ameliorate this exceptionality.

Being born here in America doesn't make you an American. Why, if birth made you American, you wouldn't need legislation, you wouldn't need any amendments to the Constitution, you wouldn't be faced with civil-rights filibustering in Washington, D.C., right now. They don't have to pass civil-rights legislation to make a Polack an American.[2]

From a perspective of political philosophy generally and democratic theory specifically it is the relationship to the "other" that is important to frame in its exceptionality. Here I am leaning upon the implication of Rancière's *Ten Theses on Politics* by putting pressure on the possibility of a figure excluded even from the logic of the second thesis which posits: "What is specific to politics is the existence of a subject defined by its participation in contraries. Politics is a paradoxical form of action."[3] And the fifth: "The people is a supplementary existence that inscribes the count of the uncounted, or part of those who have no part – that is, in the last instance, the equality of speaking beings without which inequality is inconceivable."[4] What Rancière perceives here is that democracy, by its nature, requires that there be those outside of its logic in order to establish the separation between citizen and non-citizen, or inside and outside. Where Malcolm X advances the thinking of Rancière is to understand that there is an additional space of inclusion that further defines a democratic project that understands itself as progressing a system of racial superiority rendering "citizen" normatively "white" and non-citizen coincident with Black and in need of further definition in order to provide for inclusion. What Rancière sees as "the part of no part," Malcolm X further clarifies with respect to Black bodies by finding them included within the part but in that inclusion understood to be "no-part of that part." Resident but not citizen. Subject to the law but not beneficiary of its positive logics. Included in being excluded from the "part of no part." Malcolm X understands this to be a form of foundational and devastating immorality on the part of the project of American democracy. What that means for Malcolm X is that a desire for civil rights in that context is useless in form and content. He asserts in the first speech under consideration the following:

Don't change the white man's mind – you can't change his mind, and that whole thing about appealing to the moral conscience of America. America's conscience is bankrupt. She lost all conscience a long time ago. Uncle Sam has no conscience. They don't know what morals are. They don't try and eliminate an evil because it's evil, or because it's illegal, or because it's immoral; they eliminate it only when it threatens their existence. So you're wasting your time appealing to the moral conscience of a bankrupt man like Uncle Sam.[5]

This notion of moral bankruptcy is not just rhetorical: it is the key to unlocking what can be framed as the "First Step" in Malcolm X's progress toward human rights as the *sine qua non* of establishing the Black body as emancipated from the tethers of coercive, subaltern national belonging. What has been exposed here is the central paradox that was discussed in the Introduction, through thinking with Audre Lorde's concerns with "the master's tools."[6] Malcolm X is setting up a binary that really functions as a cause and effect relationship and even further an "Or Else" with respect to the praxis of radical politics. The complexity of his argument speaks to a robust understanding of the power of the Black vote to the extent that whites abandon their predisposition to use Black votes to progress their agenda, which is to continue with their practices of marginalization. He understands this to be the result of the continuation of polices in the south that restrict Black voters' rights and lead to the empowerment of southern politicians who are dedicated to maintaining practices of segregation.

> The Dixiecrats in Washington, D.C., control the key committees that run the government. The only reason the Dixiecrats control these committees is because they have seniority. The only reason they have seniority is because they come from states where Negroes can't vote. This is not even a government that's based on democracy. It is not a government that is made up of representatives of the people. Half of the people in the South can't vote. Eastland is not even supposed to be in Washington. Half of the senators and congressmen who occupy these key positions in Washington, D.C., are there illegally, are there unconstitutionally.
>
> These senators and congressmen actually violate the constitutional amendments that guarantee the people of that particular state or county the right to vote. And the Constitution itself has within it the machinery to expel any representative from a state where the voting rights of the people are violated. You don't even need new legislation ... In fact, when you expel them, you don't need new legislation, because they will be replaced by black representatives from counties and districts where the black man is in the majority, not in the minority.[7]

This requires careful consideration. There is one reading that appears to reveal Malcolm X theorizing against his own assertion of the immoral nature of white people generally and politicians specifically. Under what pretense can Malcolm X imagine that the immoral actors he is referencing would be inclined to allow the Constitution to function as if it had not been racially biased in its form and structure at its inception? He does not believe that any such thing will happen and it is this understanding that fuels his rejection of the discourse of civil rights as the means by which Black people achieve political viability. What he means is that this reticence in and of itself on the part of the white ruling class to follow its own rules in abstract fashion, meaning without artificially demarcating the boundaries of democratic participation, makes the case for the insufficiency of the structures of American democracy and therefore a higher authority needs to be employed to work toward a solution. "Higher power" is used here advisedly and speaks to the international nature, at its most fundamental level, of Malcolm X's radical political project as well as its placement within the intellectual genealogy of social contract theory. An exemplar of what I am proposing is found in the opening moments of Jefferson's Declaration of Independence, after he lays out the foundational logic: "… it becomes necessary for one people to dissolve the political bands which have connected them with another, and to assume the powers of the earth, the separate and equal station to which the Laws of Nature and of Nature's God entitle them …"; this observation proves useful in that he proposes that the assaults on reason allow the dismantling of the offending system of governance. The document continues:

> That whenever any Form of Government becomes destructive of these ends, it is the Right of the People to alter or to abolish it, and to institute new Government, laying its foundation on such principles and organizing its powers in such form, as to them shall seem most likely to effect their Safety and Happiness.[8]

Like Malcolm X, Jefferson proposes that the abuses endured by an aggrieved people require them to establish a sovereign existence and that political structure fits into and is recognized by the larger system of political belonging that is the interlocking system of nation-states. Further, it is the unique nature of the democratic project inaugurated with the 1776 Declaration that situates the United States as an exemplar of the proper form of the modern state that renders it particularly susceptible to international pressure in two ways. The first is the notion of marginalizing the possibility of the United States situating itself as a beacon of the democratic ideal while at the same time treating its own "citizens" in reprehensible fashion. The second is, as usual in the thinking of Malcolm X, related to the first. The fact of the mistreatment of African–Americans by the United States government creates, as we have identified, a class of maligned political subject. This class represents a single body that experiences the pain and triumphs of each component of the organism mutually and represents the vanguard of the revolution.

The first component of the intellectual innovation behind the formation of this revolutionary organism is the expansion of the term Black to be roughly analogous to our current political context's employment of the term the "Global South." Malcolm X develops this idea in the text of "The Black Revolution."

> 1964 will see the Negro revolt evolve and merge into the world-wide black revolution that has been taking place on this earth since 1945. The so-called revolt will become a real black revolution. Now the black revolution has been taking place in Africa and Asia and Latin America; when I say black, I mean non-white – black, brown, red or yellow. Our brothers and sisters in Asia, who were colonized by the Europeans, our brothers and sisters in Africa, who were colonized by the Europeans, and in Latin America, the peasants who were colonized by the Europeans, have been involved in a struggle since 1945 to get the colonialists, or the colonizing powers, the Europeans, off their land, out of their country.[9]

Establishing "Black" as a status of revolutionary being in the same way that the proletariat is situated in the thinking of Karl Marx is critical to Malcolm X's system of thought. Not only is he establishing the revolutionary Black subject as transnational but also rendering the status expansive enough to allow it to encompass others who have suffered at the hands of European-based systems of oppression. This, in the thinking of Malcolm X, is not a source of melancholia or a signal of subjects mired in a particular form of victimhood. On the contrary, in the same way that Marxism situates class belonging as a point of departure for the wholesale alteration of the world system, Malcolm X witnesses the plight of the "so-called Negro" as exemplar of the system of oppression and because of that status, the site for dismantling the system. Additionally, because of the unstable relationship of the American Negro to established systems of national belonging, the subject is situated to represent revolutionary possibility broadly defined. Malcolm X, again working through the thought of Du Bois as it relates to the incompatibility of Negro and American, pushes that logic further proposing: "... I don't even consider myself an American. If you and I were Americans, there'd be no problem."[10] Figure 9 depicts the complexity of the subjectivity considered by Du Bois.

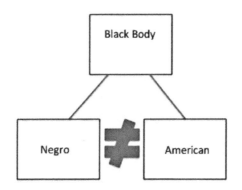

Figure 9   Du Boisian Subaltern Self-Consciousness

The feeling from Du Bois that this status of subaltern "Other" has been imposed on the Black body, and requires a certain form of self-awareness (Second-Sight), is altered here by Malcolm X. What we have here is an awareness of the consequences of systematic oppression on bodies that recognize the incompatibility of Du Bois' Negro and Malcolm's Blackness with the status of American citizenship while the same time creating an alternative system of belonging that is illustrated by Figure 10.

Substantively, and in spite of a surface reading of the fact of the matter to the contrary, Malcolm X respects the laws of the United States of America. Not only does he respect them but he also understands them to be an existential threat to the potentiality of the African–American. To the extent that he has no reason to expect that there will be a change in the morality of white people, he rejects the utility of domestic law-making in the form of civil rights to ameliorate this condition.

Civil rights comes within the domestic affairs of this country. All of our African brothers and our Asian brothers and our Latin American brothers cannot open their mouths and interfere in the domestic

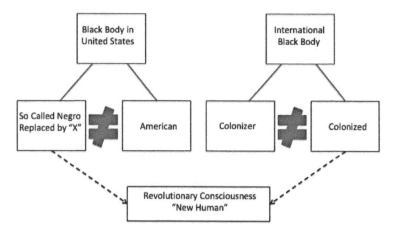

Figure 10   Malcolm X's Revolutionary Self-Consciousness

affairs of the United States. And as long as it's civil rights, this comes under the jurisdiction of Uncle Sam.

But the United Nations has what's known as the charter of human rights, it has a committee that deals in human rights. You may wonder why all of the atrocities that have been committed in Africa and in Hungary and in Asia and in Latin America are brought before the UN, and the Negro problem is never brought before the UN. This is part of the conspiracy.

Civil rights keeps you under his restrictions, under his jurisdiction. Civil rights keeps you in his pocket. Civil rights means you're asking Uncle Sam to treat you right. Human rights are your God-given rights. Human rights are the rights that are recognized by all nations of this earth. And any time anyone violates your human rights, you can take them to the world court.[11]

It is important to note here that Malcolm X is not describing human rights in the sense that they appear as relative abstractions related to natural law in social contract theory. He is interested in the specific elements of the United Nations Declaration of Human Rights from 1948. There is a way in which the entire Declaration can be admitted into evidence here as the context for Malcolm X's intention to alter the point of conflict with the system of governance from the domestic to the international. The Preamble of the document asserts the recognition of the "... inherent dignity and inalienable rights of all members of the human family is the foundation of freedom, justice and peace in the world ..." Before focusing on specific articles of the Charter it is useful to understand the cause and effect relationship illuminated here that informs the argument for revolutionary fervor on the part of the marginalized political subject. The Charter argues that the humane treatment of each and every human actor is the "foundation of ... peace in the world." What this implies is that chaos and conflict find their foundation in the denial of the recognition of the humanity of all putatively human beings. Therefore, it follows that the disruption of peace is not only caused by, but perhaps properly responded to, with chaos. We have trod this ground before, but it is important to reiterate the imperative of extracting the "so-called Negro" from the status of sub-human or quasi-human actor. To be human is to be in possession of ontological dignity and therefore recognition as a political actor in possession of human rights. From this position, several Articles of the Charter bear closer examination in support of the international law case Malcolm X is intent on making for the African–American.

Specifically, I am interested in focusing on Articles 1, 2, 6 and 7. Article 1 asserts that all humans are "born free and equal in dignity and rights." It is fairly obvious how this fits into the *longue durée* of the thinking of Malcolm X in that the appearance of the subject that preoccupies his thought first appears as a politicized subject lacking in personal agency under conditions of enslavement. The recognition of the freedom that attends the status of "human," without further qualification, allows this subject to be protected under the aegis of the UN Declaration. If we imagine that the abolition of slavery seems to ameliorate the base conditions of Article 1 it is important that the body that is human finds itself protected from marginalization based upon other factors. Article 2 deals with this condition asserting that:

Everyone is entitled to all the rights and freedoms set forth in this Declaration, without distinction of any kind, such as race, colour, sex, language, religion, political or other opinion, national or social origin, property, birth or other status. Furthermore, no distinction shall be made on the basis of the political, jurisdictional or international status of the country or territory to which a person belongs, whether it be independent, trust, non-self-governing or under any other limitation of sovereignty.

As important as the first elements of this article are for subjects who have been harmed, based upon the characteristics enumerated in the text, the second sentence is perhaps more critical for this thinking, in that it establishes the possibility of recognizing subjects independent of national belonging. This is a complex reading of this clause, but it fits within the boundaries of the understanding of bodies as political spaces that I have presented as fundamental to the thinking of Malcolm X. Malcolm X would likely alter this clause to read as follows: *Furthermore, no distinction shall be made on the basis of the political, jurisdictional, or international status of the person/body in question, whether it be independent, trust, non-self-governing or under any other limitation of sovereignty.* The alteration of the text allows for the protection of bodies that represent the extension of the logic of Rancière's "part of no part" to those who are disavowed by the national boundaries that surround and give political existence to their corporeality. This disavowal prevents the aggrieved from achieving political recognition through the civil rights accorded the citizens of the state in question because of their marginal status and further creates a double-bind in that it substantively blocks access to international jurisprudence. By positing that the body can "decouple" itself from the state that marginalizes it, and further broadening the language of Article 2 to allow for the *de facto* stateless actor to function as a self-authorizing political formation, the marginalized subject finds a mechanism that facilitates access to the protections of the 1948 Declaration.

To continue to push this logic based upon the thinking of Malcolm X is to understand the imperative of "Transnational National Belonging" that creates a "belt and suspenders" superstructure of political subjectivity for the subjects under consideration. If marginalized political subjects inside of an internationally recognized state, i.e. the "so-called Negro" in the United States of America, can be understood, under the terms of Article 2, to be under limitation of sovereignty, and can then employ that status to find belonging, in diasporic fashion, to another recognized state that grants the subject full citizenship, the aggrieved has expanded the terms and conditions of political subjectivity within the state that has subjugated them in the first place. First, as harmed as a condition of being human and eligible for the protections of the Declaration, and second as a citizen of a recognized state that offers another established form of protection. Article 6 aids this line of reasoning proclaiming that, "[e]veryone has the right to recognition everywhere as a person before the law."

Article 6 does not require citizenship in a state as a precondition to recognition in every nation-state as a juridical subject in the positive sense of the term. Malcolm X is fully aware that the "so-called Negro" is a legal subject, but only in the punitive sense of that relation rather than with respect to legal protection. The fact that the "so-called Negro" is not given the full protection of the law functions two ways in this philosophical system. First, by demanding that the United Nations force the United States to correct this behavior and second, allowing access for this demand in spite of the condition of subjective erasure with respect to access to legal protection. Article 7 serves as the final element of this legal argument, as it asserts the following:

> All are equal before the law and are entitled without any discrimination to equal protection of the law. All are entitled to equal protection against any discrimination in violation of this Declaration and against any incitement to such discrimination.

Malcolm X recognizes that the UN is the venue in which it is most appropriate to address the concerns of Black Americans. The problem that follows is the manner in which the subject in question is able to get its case to the UN for adjudication. This problem harkens back to that of sequentiality, illuminated at the beginning of this book, where, when pressed on his seeming abandonment of the Back to Africa Movement, Malcolm X gestures at the effective, if not "proper," sequence of things. This question is substantively resolved in the thought of Malcolm X through careful examination of the "or" in the speech "The Ballot *or* the Bullet." First it is important to note the expansive nature of the ballot in this philosophical system. He states unequivocally and succinctly that "[b]y ballot I only mean freedom."[12] With that explanation, we understand that the title of the speech is properly rendered "Freedom or the Bullet." Here, Malcolm X articulates a coherent "Or Else" to the continued marginalization of African–Americans, stating simply that if "freedom," broadly understood, is represented by unfettered and substantive access to the franchise, but is not available, violence is the only answer. Apparently, Malcolm X seems convinced that the ability to elect representatives and in so doing restructure the legislative branch by removing the bigots from the south who populate the "Dixiecrat" wing of the Democratic Party, would facilitate the fair representation of the interests of Black people while fracturing the power base of white supremacy in the south.

There is more here. Malcolm X is fully aware that the oppression of Black people is not a phenomenon unique to the south and emphasizes that the intelligent employment of the franchise is the key to altering the terms and conditions of Black political identity. He points to the power of the Black vote and specifically references the deleterious effect of employing it without a thought to its strategic value:

> It was the black man's vote that put the present administration in Washington, D.C. Your vote, your dumb vote, your ignorant vote, your wasted vote put in an administration in Washington, D.C., that has seen fit to pass every kind of legislation imaginable, saving you until last, the filibustering on top of that.[13]

The next step in tracing this cause and effect proposal for a form of practical politics to be practiced *in situ* by the marginalized is to interrogate the "Or Else," the "bullet," called for here. Again, Malcolm is definitive on the process that leads to the "Or Else," proposing:

> That's why, in 1964, it's time now for you and me to become more politically mature and realize what the ballot is for; what we're supposed to get when we cast a ballot; and if we don't cast a ballot, it's going to end up in a situation where we're going to have to cast a bullet.[14]

As proposed at the beginning of this chapter, Malcolm X has been, reductively, understood to be a proponent of the employment of violence as an inevitable stage in any practical political project. If nothing else is accomplished with this book, I would hope that it would dismantle categorically that assertion and demonstrate that Malcolm X has expanded the definition of political violence in important and productive ways. This is exemplified by the fact that the "Or Else" here, the "Bullet" that Malcolm X is threatening to cast at the United States for continued marginalization of freedom, is first the sanction of the United Nations. This is not to launch a campaign that substantively "defangs" the thought of Malcolm X by proposing that violence is metaphorical. That is also not true. Malcolm X has a very utilitarian vision of the utility of violence in many ways exemplified by his understanding of the Second Amendment and the notion of personal protection at the level of the individual.

> The only thing that I've ever said is that in areas where the government has proven itself either unwilling or unable to defend the lives and property of Negroes, it's time for Negroes to defend themselves. Article number two of the constitutional amendments provides for you and me the right to own a rifle or shotgun. It is constitutionally legal to own a shotgun or rifle ... If the white man doesn't want the black man buying rifles and shotguns, then let the government do its job.[15]

This assertion, in the concluding moments in "The Ballot or the Bullet" is meant to signal the possibility of the "Bloodless Revolution" that Malcolm X will expose in the text of "The Black Revolution." As a practical matter, the first place to begin is with the operative term here, "Revolution," that Malcolm X carefully modifies as "Black" and further as "bloodless," as opposed to "French," "American," "Russian," "Chinese," etc. which continues his practice of blurring to the point of erasure or sublation the notion of national identity as opposed to Blackness. In taking up the question of revolution as a unit of analysis, one is naturally led to Bernard Yack's text, *The Longing for Total Revolution*, where the opening paragraphs propose the following:

> There are moments in our lives when we cannot help but be filled with disgust at the dangerous, vulgar, and unruly aspects of human society. At these moments, we long to escape the limitations of our social existence. Since such sentiments are probably coeval with civilized life, it is not surprising to discover that there has been a longing for social transformation in every culture and every historical epoch. On the other hand, the intensity, direction, and impact of this longing vary enormously from one epoch and culture to another. The longing for social transformation can manifest itself as a gentle nostalgia for a distant past or a violent yearning for the Apocalypse; it can focus on particular objects and institutions or make us uneasy with all of our social relationships; it can provide an individual with a pleasant diversion or inspire mass movements.
> This study seeks to define and account for a specifically modern form of universal longing for social transformation ... There is little

doubt that since the French Revolution, European intellectuals have been prone to especially intense and violent longings for social transformation ...[16]

This preoccupation with the violence that populates revolutionary social change, which Yack proposes is a central element of the thinking of "European intellectuals," is altered here by Malcolm X. This establishes an interesting binary system of "Thinking Revolution" that sets the terms and conditions of the desire for social change on the part of radical black thought and the resistance to that advance by structures of white supremacy. To the extent that societal order, in the minds of European intellectuals, is altered through violence (law constituting violence) and the status secured by law maintaining violence, it is natural to understand that radical politics that extends itself to the point of revolutionary societal destabilization must include acts of violence. The argument that Malcolm X seems to be making is that the Declaration of Human Rights and the notion that the United Nations would be in a position to hold a sovereign state accountable for violations is in fact both a destabilizing and a law-establishing form of violence. This is predicated on the belief that the project of nation-states formed and maintained through the ethos of white supremacy are ontologically violent and to interrupt that logic is a form of disruptive coercive force, particularly in that the phenomenon is derived from juridical systems. Malcolm X clearly leans on the "idea" of democracy, rather than its praxis in the United States, to propose why the state is uniquely situated to alter itself through an act of revolutionary social change that does not require "blood." He proposes the following in the text of "The Black Revolution":

Why is America in a position to bring about a bloodless revolution? Because the Negro in this country holds the balance of power and if the Negro in this country were given what the Constitution says he is supposed to have, the added power of the Negro in this country would sweep all of the racists and segregationists out of office. It would wipe out the Southern segregationism that now controls America's foreign policy, as well as America's domestic policy.

And the only way without bloodshed that this can be brought about is that the black man has to be given full use of the ballot in every one of the fifty states. But if the black man doesn't get the ballot, then you are going to be faced with another man who forgets the ballot and starts using bullets.[17]

Malcolm X again flattens the relationship between international and domestic relations as it relates to the political life of the "so-called Negro," proposing that "Southern segregationism" as a system of thought is implicated in the framing of policy both foreign and domestic. This formulation emulates the language of the Oath of Allegiance sworn by members of the government to protect the Constitution against "enemies foreign and domestic." By framing the Southern relationship to the marginalization of Black people specifically, as indiscernible from the foreign policy toward the Global South, or Malcolm X's framing of all victims of European colonial violence as "Black," is to contextualize further the claim of the essential nature of internationalism to this system of thought by understanding that in his mind there is no productive way to disaggregate the two. This is important and allows us to revisit the new subject formed in the imaginary of Malcolm X, what I have labeled the "New Human" (a product of revolutionary consciousness) as a transnational actor that can pick from the "menu" of legal and coercive apparatus for the punishment and/or accountability of nation-states in order to secure their future politically, socially and economically. The final term here relates to the imperative of dealing with the "economic" as a discrete element of the thinking of Malcolm X.

The theory and practice of revolution would be incomplete without an effort to understand the position of the "economic" in this project of dismantling the formal structures of an oppressive regime. It is clear that Malcolm X is calling for a political and social notion of collectivity and, as mentioned earlier, establishing "Black" as a form of revolutionary being and awareness that situates class as a secondary consideration to matters of race. In the thinking of Malcolm X, race, or Blackness as a product of colonial oppression, overlays the class of the subject in question, rendering traditional Marxist categories only partially useful in analyzing this system of thought.

Cedric Robinson explores this in great detail in the canonical text *Black Marxism: The Making of the Black Radical Tradition*. Robinson is led to believe that the Black radical tradition that fueled movements against slavery was based upon the recovery of identity in spite of "the intellectual weight and authority of the official European version of the past."[18] This system of Black radical epistemologies leads to the framing of Black Nationalism as a category of thought that Malcolm X particularizes in the manner explored in this text and that has its own economic philosophy.

> The economic philosophy of black nationalism is pure and simple. It only means that we should control the economy of our community ...
>
> So the economic philosophy of black nationalism means in every church, in every civic organization, in every fraternal order, it's time now for our people to become conscious of the importance of controlling the economy of our community. If we own the stores, if we operate the businesses, if we try and establish some industry in our own community, then we're developing to the position where we are creating employment for our own kind.[19]

This is not anti-capitalist thought, but it is also not anti-Marxist either, in the sense that Robinson reveals that Black Nationalism questions the efficacy of capitalism as a force for positive subject formation and Malcolm X seems to be proposing some hybrid system. What that seems to portend is the employment of Marxist categories of revolutionary societal change through the consciousness of the masses that creates a socialism of opportunity that allows for something like capitalist accumulation internal to that system. This substantively completes the logic of the non-geographically dependent nationalism that creates the possibility of transnational subjectivity but also transnational control of capital for the benefit of the radical political project and its adherents. Malcolm X had grave concerns about the viability of global capitalism as a result of its excesses. In an interview in the *Young Socialist* in 1965 he is asked, "[w]hat is your opinion of the world-wide struggle now going on between capitalism and socialism?" He responded:

> It is impossible for capitalism to survive, primarily because the system of capitalism needs some blood to suck. Capitalism used to be like an eagle, but now it's more like a vulture. It used to be strong enough to go and suck anybody's blood whether they were strong or not. But now it has become more cowardly, like the vulture, and it can only suck the blood of the helpless. As the nations of the world free themselves, then capitalism has less victims, less to suck, and it becomes weaker and weaker. It's only a matter of time in my opinion before it will collapse completely.[20]

As a practical matter, Malcolm X had a fraught relationship with economics broadly understood, in that at no point in his intellectual development could he get capital to "work" for him. In fact, one of the elements that must be considered salient to the notion promoted by Jamil Al-Amin, mentioned at the outset of this book, was the notion of Malcolm X's unimpeachable integrity: there is no evidence that he ever profited from his efforts on behalf of the marginalized. Malcolm X understood the need for money and financial support of his efforts; that is obvious. His concern on this point maps against his gloss on the term "segregation" that was about control not separation. On the economic side of doing social justice work he was explicitly willing to accept financial support from virtually any quarter but was concerned that he (1) understood where the money originated and (2) what the implications of the acceptance of the capital might prove to be.

One might posit from this, when considering how capital is situated in this philosophical system at some remove from the set of central concerns, that Malcolm X privileges the possession of a positive relation to the self as a more valuable currency than currency. Succinctly, Malcolm X does not view the practice of radical humanistic subjectivity as *transactional*. There is no room in his philosophical system to witness justice as being related to compensation, meaning that it is impossible for him to imagine his central concern of police brutality being ameliorated by an attempt at establishing a system of justice that compensates the victims of this violence. This erects, at least, a theoretical firewall around this philosophical system, to protect it from being compromised by "selling out" to the highest bidder.

The other component of Malcolm X's theory of revolution is religion. We dealt with this in a previous chapter, but it is important to ensure that proper emphasis has been placed on the revolutionary potentiality of religion in this system. It could be argued that religion (Islam), in the political practice of Malcolm X, is an end to the means of achieving social justice and personal political sovereignty, rather than a practice for the sake of personal redemption. This is not to undermine the importance of religion, or perhaps more appropriately theology, in this system of thought, but to view it as an organizing principle rather than as one of a number of factors that can cause debilitating division. That being said, it is important to recognize the elements of the practice of Islam, whether the version espoused by the Nation of Islam, or more orthodox practice, for its contribution to dismantling the context of subaltern existence.

The French Revolution is a useful foil for pursuing this line of reasoning. French revolutionary thought, as practiced by the Committee of Public Safety, sought to destabilize the political and social existence of the French citizen by altering the terms and conditions of relating oneself to the state, others and the world at large. This is obvious in the establishment of the revolutionary calendar that altered the relationship of the individual to the continuum of time, in that the beginning of political subjectivity instantiated itself at the revolutionary moment. Along with this political awakening was the status of citizen, which was meant to refuse the imperatives of subjectivity explicit in the relationship of the individual to the monarch. By executing Louis XVI, but only after dismantling the divinity of the sovereign by renaming him Louis Capet, the revolutionary council required new modalities of the practice of governance. What remained intact were the borders of France, rendering concrete the Frenchness of the French Revolution and perhaps restricting the progress of this logic beyond these national borders.

I want to emphasize here the manner in which the elements of Islam discussed earlier in many respects mirror important aspects of the logic of the French Revolution while at the same time exceeding the boundaries of that event's ambition. As a practical matter I am focused on the revolutionary potential of alternative temporality and its relationship to the formation of a radical historiography. This establishes Islam as positing, for its adherents, an alternative and internally coherent sense of time: what I am marking as an essential element of a revolutionary political project. But what is important to underscore here in closing this chapter is to witness the manner in which structures of power, in this instance, white supremacy, understand categorically incremental motions whose *telos* is the disruption of this totalizing perspective.

I raised this point in the closing sections of the chapter on the body, where we witnessed the inevitable death of Malcolm X. I mean *inevitable* in the sense that his non-violent advocacy for the cessation of violence visited upon innocent African–Americans is understood by white supremacist logic as itself violent. There is a way in which this can be labeled as a form of cognitive dissonance on the part of established power whose foundational ethos is the necessity of white people (and here it is important to understand this as patriarchal at the same instance) to remain at the top of this hierarchical societal order. The problem with that characterization, and I believe that Malcolm X perceives this, is that it misses the essential internal logic that must be confronted. It is *not* that non-violent protests are perceived as violent by white supremacists because of a pathological inability to witness the truth. It is that non-violent protests do violence to their system of knowing and are therefore necessarily understood as violent to their system of Being. Malcolm X understands that white supremacy, and here we can effectively substitute American democracy, is completely violent in its inextricable relationship to the system of empire and colonialism. In effect, the exhortation by Fanon in his *Wretched of the Earth*, that:

> [C]olonialism is not a machine capable of thinking, a body endowed with reason. It is naked violence and only gives in when confronted with greater violence.[21]

Where Malcolm X advances the thinking of Fanon here, and this is perhaps an inevitable alteration based upon the differences in the phenomena observed by these two thinkers, is to witness the necessity of understanding non-violence as violence in the perception of colonial/American power. This responds to the important revelation by Yack that all revolution is viewed through the violence and dystopia of the French Revolution. What this means for the thinking of Malcolm X is that he is forced to qualify his revolutionary notion of Black people being empowered to vote as "Bloodless" to mark that it will be perceived as violent and that it is *de facto* violent in that it tends to decenter if not dismantle the dominant worldview. This resolves while at the same time recertifies the primary difficulty in examining the thought of Malcolm X that tends to be overwhelmed by the idea that he is espousing a system of violent and futile confrontation between Black and white in America – if not, as we have seen, on a planetary basis.

This is why, in the opening sections of this chapter, I proposed that there could be a way in which Malcolm X's philosophy of revolution is not a discreet element of his philosophical system, just as I have tried to separate, for instance, his understanding of ontology for examination. All roads lead to revolution because each element is, in and of itself, revolutionary, and each element, from (re)naming, to understanding the Black body to be valuable and beautiful, understood, recognized and attacked as violent.

Conclusion

What I have attempted to do here has been to follow carefully the threads of Malcolm X's thought with the foundational principle being that his "activism" functions in a symbiotic relationship with his philosophical system. I have used the term "system" here primarily to emphasize that Malcolm X's thought has a coherent relationship to what I have established as distinct "parts" in order to trace a path through it. To put it plainly, the system begins with questions of ontology, asking quite simply where did the subjects that interest him come from? This is clearly a fraught question for the Negro that is inexplicably related to the bodies that were stolen from Africa and forced to labor for the creation of a country upon threat of corporeal death. These bodies, as political actors, exist in a particular space that is generally but not necessarily delineated by sovereign national boundaries. The final movement in this thinking is to understand the practice of radical politics, revolution, that is designed to fracture the logic of the system that has delivered the subject to the necessity of this activity in order to establish new political perceptions.

The circular nature of Malcolm X's system is an important element to mark in service of being in a position to productively grapple with the evolutionary nature of his thought as well as the implication of something like sequentiality internal to his radical political project. This requires elaboration.

It would be a mistake to propose that I understand the thought of Malcolm X as teleological in the manner in which this text proceeds: flowing necessarily from considerations of ontology to terminus in revolution. What seems to be the case is that these represent categories of thought for Malcolm X, and within each category, all four of the elements operate in order to resolve the implicit tension. The tension being the necessity of considering any discreet element of what I have proposed here, without "thinking" the other elements simultaneously. This poses a challenge for sketching this system of knowing in the written form we find most readily accessible, but actually renders the employment of this system in radical politics coherent. This allows us to understand the biographical claim that Malcolm X is in a process of continued evolution that cycles through several phases of being that are well-trodden ground from an historical perspective. What this portends from a philosophical perspective is that these points of transition are related to the progress of this philosophical thought as it moves from one artificially delineated phase to the next. This establishes a form of radical temporality for this thinking that is definitively non-linear in the sense that life is not.

This elision of the necessity of linearity and sequentiality – something like, if a group does this, then that, they should follow up by doing x in order to get to y and finally arrive at a solution that looks like z – is not what I believe is going on here. This system of thought is sufficiently pliant to accommodate changing circumstances that are principally related to the manner in which established regimes of power fight subjective alteration and destabilization of political systems. I want to point out here that there is always the question of what the revolution must learn about itself in order to continue its forward momentum. This is much about the context or structures against which radical political action exerts its force and in turn receives often unpredictable "feedback" that obviates the course of action that may have seemed apparent until circumstances change. This is obvious in observing the manner in which Malcolm X never seemed reluctant to allow experience to alter his perception of the way forward. As a practical matter, this thinking returns us to where this book begins, with Malcolm X pushing on the question regarding a return to Africa by rendering it dependent upon several layers of intellectual evolution that are broadly defined as Black Minded. In other words, a return to the geographic spatiality of Africa is an aspirational goal that need not be realized for the effort to be successful. In some sense I have convinced myself through this exercise that at the end of the day, the proper descriptor for this system of radical political thought and philosophy is simply: *Black Minded*. This speaks to the problem for the practice of naming or categorizing the thought that has been presented here. The political philosophy of Malcolm X may in fact best be described as the philosophy of revolution of Malcolm X, not just in its breadth and depth of consideration but in its reception into the imaginary of the world. Hence a particular form of "Mindedness." Like gravity, it doesn't matter if you believe in it or not, it is always there. And further, the aspirational nature requires a new way of thinking and perceiving the world around you. There is an important analogy to gravity here that can be understood to be both blessing and curse. Roughly put, it holds things to the Earth and also keeps them from flying away into oblivion. There is a way in which the appeal of the philosophical system of Malcolm X is understood in this manner.

In 1963 Kenneth Clark interviewed James Baldwin and allowed the writer to articulate his manifold concerns regarding the "appeal" of Malcolm X's message to the youth in particular. Baldwin proposed the following:

> What Malcolm tells them, in effect, is that they should be proud of being black, and God knows that they should be. That is a very important thing to hear in a country which assures you that you should be ashamed of it. Of course, in order to do this, what he does is destroy a truth and invent a history. *What he does is say, "you're better because you're black." Well, of course that isn't true. That's the trouble* [my italics].
>
> I don't think – to put it as simply as I can, without trying now to investigate whatever the motives of any given Muslim leader may be – it is the only movement in the country, that you can call grass roots – I hate to say that, but it's true, because it is only – when Malcolm talks or one of the Muslims talks, they articulate for all the Negro people who hear them, who listen to them. They articulate their suffering, the suffering which has been in this country so long denied. That's Malcolm's great authority over any of his audiences. He corroborates their reality; he tells them that they really exist. You know?
>
> It is much more sinister because it is much more effective. It is much more effective, because it is, after all, comparatively easy to invest a population with a false morale by giving them a false sense of superiority, and it will always break down in a crisis. It's the history of Europe, simply – it's one of the reasons that we are in this terrible place. It is one of the reasons that we have five cops standing on the back of a woman's neck in Birmingham, because at some point they believed, they were taught and they believed, that they were better than other people because they were white. It leads to a moral bankruptcy. It is inevitable, it cannot but lead there.
>
> But my point here is that the country is for the first time worried about the Muslim movement. It shouldn't be worried about the Muslim movement. That's not the problem. The problem is to eliminate the conditions which breed the Muslim movement.[1]

There is much to unpack here. My primary concern is to focus on Baldwin's correct perception of the core of Malcolm's system (what he understands as something like popular appeal) is to reify the positive existence of the self. His concern is the employment of what he understands to be the lie that Black people are better, if not ontologically, then as a product of their suffering. Baldwin understands this to be wholly invested in a genus of "Supremacy," of which "white" or "European" is a species, and therefore he frames what we have derived here as the gravitational pull of Malcolm's Black Mindedness as inevitably totalitarian and morally bankrupt. From that position, one can better understand the detail of a discussion, framed as a debate, between Malcolm X and Baldwin in September of 1963, in which the author approaches this same concern from a different quarter.

In this segment, Baldwin situates his own refutation of organized religion and the notion of subject-defining faith as the troubling element of this thinking that creates an identity based upon mythology. Baldwin goes further and proposes that the only way in which this cascading problematic of "competing supremacies" can be eradicated is through the lack of discernible and particular racial identity on the planet. Malcolm X, of course, rejects the premise of losing Blackness as a source, or perhaps even the foundation, of his subjectivity. This is the form and content of the problem of being Black Minded, a problem that Malcolm X understands as beneficial in that it could potentially lead to the expulsion of Black people from the national and geographic locus of the destruction of their identity. Baldwin's understanding, if not fear, is that this framework, again, what he calls "authority," will become the foundation of the way in which Black youth will frame their politics and lead to catastrophe. I believe that, like gravity, Malcolm X's system of subjective recovery in fact becomes the dominant system of radical political thought: the manner in which this system has receded into the DNA of understanding of Black radical politics is instructive. The text *Black Power: The Politics of Liberation*, by Kwame Ture, *née* Stokely Carmichael, and Charles V. Hamilton, exemplifies what I am describing here. The text, written in 1967, includes the following canonical statement early in the first chapter, "White Power: The Colonial Situation":

To put it another way, there is no "American dilemma" because black people in this country form a colony, and it is not in the interest of the colonial power to liberate them. Black people are legal citizens of the

United States with, for the most part, the same *legal* rights as other citizens. Yet they stand as colonial subjects in relation to white society. This institutional racism has another name: colonialism.[2]

This is unquestionably a coherent recast of the thinking Malcolm X exposed several years before and upon multiple occasions that we have carefully traced in this text. Further, Ture and Hamilton write as follows in the second chapter, "Black Power: Its Need and Substance":

> To do this, we must first redefine ourselves. Our basic need is to reclaim our history and our identity from what must be called cultural terrorism, from the depredation of white guilt. We shall have to struggle for the right to create our own terms through which to define ourselves and our relationship to society, and to have these terms recognized. This is the first necessity of a free people, and the first right that any oppressor must suspend.[3]

This is clearly directly related to the thinking we have explored here with respect to the emphasis Malcolm X places on his understanding of ontology and its relationship to positive subject-hood. One simply cannot properly place these canonical expressions regarding the critical elements of what Ture and Hamilton understand as "Black Power" without dealing with Malcolm X. However, when one examines the index you will find thinkers that include George Washington Carver, Du Bois, Fanon, John Hope Franklin, E. Franklin Frazier, King, Machiavelli, Morgenthau, Nkrumah, Bayard Rustin, Booker T. Washington, Woodrow Wilson and Whitney M. Young, Jr. There is literally no mention of Malcolm X in the main text, and it is not until the republication of the text a quarter of a century later that Ture mentions him in the new Afterword, writing in 1992:

> Malcolm X had said just before his assassination that the U.S.A. could avoid violent Revolution; perhaps. Revolutionaries do not take the path of spilling blood easily. But Malcolm's statement is no longer true despite the fact that U.S. capitalism has been doing everything to make it so.[4]

In the revised edition, neither Ture nor Hamilton attempts to make explicit the reliance upon categories elaborated by Malcolm X. I do not view this as a failing, but rather the most coherent exemplar of the ubiquity of the philosophical system of Malcolm X in the Black radical tradition.

This speaks clearly to what can perhaps best be properly characterized as the internally coherent and self-sufficient nature of each individual element explored here that can "succeed" by resolving its own logic without necessitating movement to the next phase, while at the same time opening the breach to do so when it is possible. The thought of Malcolm X represents a bridge (as mentioned earlier, from Du Bois to Fanon), while also creating a breach for improvisation around these themes that then becomes a negative space that is imperceptible in its totality. Some of this is obvious but bears articulation, particularly what I am describing of the "self-standing" nature of the elements I have identified here.

One can successfully advance the status of marginalized subjectivity by resolving the fractured historical self that is the point of focus of Malcolm X's preoccupation with ontology without traveling the entire course to a stage of revolutionary alteration of the context of "being through revolution." The same goes for a focus on the embodied nature of this philosophical system. Outside of the context of resolving questions of ontology, geographic space, and the wholesale restructuring of the system, subjects can develop a positive internal relationship with their own bodies and solve the threshold problematic of "true self-consciousness." In other words, what I have identified as the non-linearity of this system of thinking implies that each "stage" contains the essential elements of the other stages or, more carefully, the goal of each stage; in the approach adopted by Malcolm X this is a positive relationship with the self as the start and endpoint of this effort. What this thinking is meant to accomplish is to resolve the salient question of what Malcolm X accomplished with his life in some sense, but in this context specifically his thought.

The cynical case against Malcolm X can best be expressed by concerns regarding the impracticality of something like Black Nationalism when one understands nationalism to function in only one way. This seems reductive in that the manner of considering the case of Malcolm X misses the metaphysical nature of his system of thinking or in this parlance its "Black Mindedness." A return to Ture and Hamilton in *Black Power* can be understood to represent what I am proposing here when read against our earlier gloss on Foucault's notion of biopower. Ture and Hamilton define Black Power as follows:

> ... Black Power means that black people see themselves as part of a new force sometimes called the "Third World"; that we see our struggle as closely related to liberation struggles around the world. We must hook up with these struggles.[5]

This is again a recast of what I have identified as the radical internationalism proposed by Malcolm X that does not connect the relationship the thinker makes explicit to the imaginary, and a disembodiedness that is the "true" transnational power of this thinking, defying the boundaries of time and space. Further, what I mean to emphasize here is that the power of the thinking of Malcolm X is that it performs this type of disappearance in its omnipresence that is the foundation of Foucault's understanding of biopower. Much of this effort has revealed itself as a reclamation project in some sense or a process of revealing the durability of Malcolm X's thought.

The notion of reclamation needs to be qualified and contextualized. There is no conversation that I can imagine regarding the desire of Black people for political, economic and social justice that does not include Malcolm X. But my concern is that this inclusion has blunted the edge of the thinking of Malcolm X that was structurally far ahead of its time and in many ways uninterrogated. Part of this reclamation project is also bearing witness to the way in which Malcolm X has been appropriated as a subject by the popular imaginary. This relates to the conceptualization above as the way in which the opposition to positive Black subjectivity alters its approach in order to marginalize its opposition. In this vein, I wonder what Malcolm X would make of the United States Postal Service honoring him on a stamp (or more appropriately, what *we* should make of it), when the foundation of his thinking was dedicated to dismantling the very government that issued the commemorative postage. I asked my uncle, John Sawyer III, Ed. D., who was a member of the Stamp Committee when this was authorized, for some insight into what was going on at the time (1999) and how Malcolm X became the twenty-second individual to be honored in the Black Heritage Series. Dr Sawyer replied as follows:

The story behind the Malcolm X Black Heritage Stamp issued in 1999 was a decision that lends credence to the commitment that the United States of America was and can become a place where people with different diverse views and ideas can work together.

With respect to the matter you are most interested [in], the Malcolm X stamp was issued in 1999. It was one of the most popular stamps issued in the series. While there was discussion of the controversial positions Malcolm X had taken in his life, the Committee and the PMG recognized his impact and honored him with the Black Heritage stamp in 1999.[6]

There is ample reason to posit the production of this stamp as a positive development and it is interesting to note how far Public Enemy's claim, in their song "Fight the Power," that "Most of my heroes don't appear on no stamps," is no longer valid, because at least one, Malcolm X, would appear ten years after the song was written. The stamp in this instance, as a form of memorial of Malcolm X, allows us to reflect on the challenge presented by Audre Lorde and its relationship to what Malcolm X described on January 7, 1965 as being "sufficiently black-minded" to be expelled from the nation-state that marginalized Black people. The question regarding the possibility of fulfilling the project of Black political viability, in the direct understanding of Malcolm X, should necessarily have prevented actions like the production of a stamp designed to memorialize his presence as a subject dedicated to destabilizing that same state.

Conversely, in an oblique homage to the concerns of James Baldwin that the trajectory of Black positive subjectivity ends in negative typologies of supremacy, the government can frame the philosophy espoused by Malcolm X as one of a series of possible ways of being, rather than a devastating counternarrative to the entire project of the United States, broadly considered in its relationship to global white supremacy. In this vein, given that Malcolm X is not here to witness this effort and elaborate the next step, what must that alteration in this framework be? I will resist the opportunity to elaborate a twenty-first-century brand of Black Mindedness and instead acknowledge that it must be the Black Lives Matter (BLM) movement, where we witness the continued and concrete relevance of Malcolm X's philosophical system.

Some of this is perhaps obvious in that if we accept that police brutality against Black bodies is perhaps the prime motivator of Malcolm

X's radical political thought, then the BLM's emphasis on state-based violence establishes the linchpin for this argument. But there is more to unpack here and it relates itself as an elaboration of the imperative of naming on the part of Malcolm X as a totalizing proclamation of mattering. Black Lives Matter dispenses with the intellectual bankshot we traced in the ontology chapter and simply proclaims that Black lives must be respected and honored; white supremacists predictably employ the self-same playbook we witnessed in resistance to the "X" as a way of reclaiming positive identity.

The demand for advocates of Black Lives Matter to assert that they understand that (a) all lives matter and (b) that Black lives *don't* matter more than other lives, particularly those of the police, is an echo across the decades of the demand for Malcolm X to say his real name to satisfy the concerns of white people that were examined here in the clash on the "City Desk" show in 1963. One need go no further than the silent protest of professional football quarterback Colin Kaepernick to witness the durability of this depraved logic and its inextricable relationship to the thought of Malcolm X in at least four ways.

First, Kaepernick asserts that his political awakening came as a necessary response to the murder of innocent Black people at the hands of police who go unpunished and oftentimes find themselves rewarded. Second, he embarks upon a silent demonstration against this moral outrage that is reframed by white supremacists as being disrespectful of the military and a danger to national security: apparently the logic being that if the police can't kill innocent Black people, how could the nation defend itself against its enemies? Finally, the question of genealogy rears its head. Witness the following, written by someone named Clay Travis, on the website "Outkick the Coverage" under the title "Colin Kaepernick is an Idiot." After asserting that there is no evidence of anyone getting away with murder and reifying the fact that a protest against police brutality is an attack on the "troops," he asks:

> ... once you make a political statement like this your own life becomes worthy of discussion and analysis. Kaepernick was raised by two white parents after his own birth parents weren't willing or able to raise him themselves. If the country is fundamentally racist, doesn't the fact that two white people chose to raise an abandoned black child offer persuasive evidence that his analysis of the country's racial composition is overly broad and not supported by his own life experience?[7]

Many commentators followed this line of reasoning and further asserted that because Kaepernick is of mixed race he is not sufficiently "Black" to have an opinion on the lives of Black people. One can readily witness the specter of the demand to know the names of Malcolm X's parents on the set of "City Desk" in order to undermine the integrity of his protest in this accounting for the racial makeup and upbringing of Kaepernick. Finally, the relationship of Kaepernick's protest to the philosophical system of Malcolm X would not be complete without ensuring that Islamophobia is deployed by its opponents. The following exemplifies this element of the attack:

Nearly every dimension of the embattled Kaepernick's identity – from his love for country to his racial identity, the particulars about his family life to his personal relationships – have been closely scrutinized and callously attacked. Kaepernick's seated protest, which converges with proliferating anti-Islam sentiment in America, has also led some to insinuate that Islam is the catalyst spurring his "hate for America." Yes, even Kaepernick's faith is in question, during a time when Islam is perceived to be far more than a religion, but in line with a trumped-up subset of Kaepernick's detractors, a religion viewed as a threat to American values and national security.

… Delving into the quarterback's personal life, the architects of the "Kaepernick is a Muslim" narrative attributed his conversion to his romantic relationship with Hot 97s Nessa Diab – a Muslim American from the Bay Area who "has frequently spoken about perceived racial injustices and 'Islamaphobia' (sic) in the U.S." As the rumors spread further, and the contours of Kaepernick's relationship with a "Muslim activist" made more public, mainstream conservative media followed their fringe counterparts. On Tuesday, Fox News reported: "Kaepernick, who was notably photographed with Bible quotes tattooed on his biceps when he first came into the league, also posted a greeting in July acknowledging 'a lot of people' who he knew [were] fasting during the Muslim holiday of Ramadan and wishing them 'a Happy Eid!' He also was heavily critical on social media of Republican presidential candidate Donald Trump's proposed ban on Muslims."

The preeminent conservative media outlet attributed Kaepernick's racial and religious consciousness to Diab, his Muslim girlfriend. In short, Kaepernick was either Muslim by association, or a closet Muslim. Fox News injected momentum and legitimacy to the swelling belief that Kaepernick's conversion to Islam is what sparked his "political radicalism" or "hate for America."[8]

Colin Kaepernick's protest is situated in the long line of well-known athletes who used their platform to bring attention to the urgency of social justice, Muhammad Ali being the most obvious. But the point here is not to examine points of overlap, or the diversion of the efforts of Kaepernick and Ali, but rather to pay careful attention to the absolute uniformity of the response of white supremacists to the call for positive Black subjectivity. Very like black holes (which, until recently couldn't be "seen" but could be witnessed by the reaction of the phenomena that interact with them), the philosophical system of Malcolm X, "Black Minded", can be obscured. but the reaction to it cannot.

At the end of the day, it seems clear that the legacy of Malcolm X as an activist is without question, but the ambition of my work has been to identify Malcolm X's philosophical system. This allows this thinking to be traced across time and space and to find itself properly accounted for in the intellectual genealogy to which it relates itself and more often than not serves to destabilize. In this effort properly to place the thought of Malcolm X in conversation with thinkers that represent this canon, some decisions seem obvious (Du Bois, Lorde, Fanon, etc.), while others may appear reductive or perhaps unnecessarily reifying the presence of white, European male thinkers (Hegel, Sartre, etc.). This is a methodical decision on two fronts. First, in order to witness boundaries being transgressed, one might be served by knowing what those boundaries consist of; and secondly, my belief that methodologically the process of decolonizing the canon is enhanced not just by inclusion and exclusion but by accurately placing thinkers where they belong within the canon of philosophical thought.

This last chapter is a conclusion in title only. It is my sincere hope that this book will elicit further conversation on Malcolm X in particular and the systemic resonance of his work more generally.

Notes

INTRODUCTION

1. Transcription of a recording of a conversation with Jamil Abdullah Al-Amin and Michael Sawyer from March 5, 2015.
2. Malcolm X, *The Autobiography of Malcolm X: As Told to Alex Haley*. Grove Press: 1965.
3. Ozzie Davis, Eulogy of Malcolm X.
4. Marable, Manning, *A Life of Reinvention*. Viking Press: 2011.
5. Ball, Jared A. and Burroughs, Todd Steven (editors). *A Lie of Reinvention: Correcting Manning Marable's Malcolm X*. Black Classic Press: 2012, 30.
6. https://pagesix.com/2017/05/06/malcom-x-admitted-he-couldnt-sexually-satisfy-wife/ 7. Malcolm X. *By Any Means Necessary*. Pathfinder Press: 2013, 133.
8. Ibid.
9. Ibid., 134.
10. Breitman, George (editor). *Malcolm X Speaks*. Grove Press: 1965, 52.
11. Ibid., 51.
12. Ibid., 24.
13. Fredrickson, George M. *Black Liberation: A Comparative History of Black Ideologies in the United States and South Africa*. Oxford University Press: 1995, 301–2.
14. Ibid.
15. Ibid., 119.
16. Lorde, Audre. "The Master's Tools Will Never Dismantle the Master's House". *This Bridge Called My Back: Writings by Radical Women of Color*, fourth edition. Morage, Cherríe and Anzaldúa, Gloria (editors). State University of New York Press: 2015, 94.
17. Martin Luther, Jr. *Stride Toward Freedom: The Montgomery Story*. Beacon Press: 2010, 78.
18. Atwal, Sandeep S. (editor). "Speech to Peace Corps Workers." *Malcolm X: Collected Speeches, Debates and Interviews (1960–1965)*. Oulef, Org.: 497.
19. Strauss, Leo. *What is Political Philosophy? And Other Studies*. Free Press: 1959, 11–12.
20. Moten, Fred. *The Universal Machine*. Duke University Press: 2018, 8.
21. Ibid., 8–9.
22. Ibid., 3.
23. Gordon, Lewis. *Existentia Africana*. Routledge: 2000, 35.

24. Echeruo, Michael J. C. "Edward W. Blyden, 'The Jewish Question' and Diaspora: Theory and Practice". *Journal of Black Studies*, Vol. 40, No. 4, March 2010, 545.
25. Ibid.

CHAPTER 1

1. Du Bois, W. E. B. *The Souls of Black Folk*. Norton Critical Edition: 1999, 10–11.
2. Ibid., 11.
3. Ibid., 11.
4. Ibid., 11.
5. Fanon, Frantz. *Peau noire, masques blancs*. Points, Paris: 1952, 6.
6. "City Desk", March 13, 1963. My transcription.
7. Ibid.
8. Ambar, Saladin. *Malcolm X at Oxford Union: Racial Politics in a Global Era*. Oxford University Press: 2014, 73.
9. "City Desk."
10. Alter, Robert. *The Five Books of Moses: A Translation with Commentary*. Norton: 2004, 21.
11. Morrison, Toni. *Song of Solomon*. Vintage International: 2004, 17–18.
12. Muhammad, Elijah. *Message to the Black Man*. The Final Call, Inc.: 1965, 54–5.
13. Ibid.
14. Ibid., 102.

CHAPTER 2

1. Marable. *Malcolm X: A Life of Reinvention*. 209.
2. Breitman. *Malcolm X Speaks*. 8.
3. Ibid., 6.
4. Fanon, Frantz. *The Wretched of the Earth*. Grove Press: 1963, 32.
5. Ibid., 67.
6. Benjamin, Walter. "Critique of Violence". *Reflections: Essays, Aphorisms, Autobiographical Writings*. Schocken: 1978, 286.
7. https://youtu.be/vxIh_CD7Rvo My transcription of the April 27, 1962 speech.
8. Sartre, Jean-Paul. *The Transcendence of the Ego*. Hill and Wang: 1991, 40–1.
9. Ibid., 40–1.
10. Ibid., 43.
11. Ibid., 41.
12. Ibid., 44.
13. Ibid., 44.
14. Ibid., 45.
15. El-Shabazz, El-Hajj. *The Diary of Malcolm X*. Boyd, Herb and el-Shabazz, Ilyasah (editors). Third World Press: 2013, 5.

16. hooks, bell. *Outlaw Culture: Resisting Representation*. Routledge: 1994, 183.
17. Hudson-Weems, Clenora. "From Malcolm Little to El Hajj Malik El Shabazz: From Malcolm's Evolving Attitude Toward Africana Women". *The Western Journal of Black Studies*. Vol.17, No. 1, 1993, 27.
18. hooks. *Outlaw Culture*. 188.
19. Ibid., 183.
20. Breitman. *Malcolm X Speaks*. 107.
21. Patterson, Orlando. *Slavery and Social Death: A Comparative Study*. Harvard University Press: 1982, 5.
22. Ibid., 5.
23. Ibid., 10.
24. hooks. *Outlaw Culture*. 193.
25. Ibid., 193.
26. Ibid., 188.
27. Roberts, Randy and Smith, Johnny. *Blood Brothers: The Fatal Friendship Between Malcolm X and Muhammad Ali*. Basic Books: 2016.
28. My transcription.
29. Berger, Maurice. "Malcolm X as Visual Strategist". *Lens: Photography, Video, and Visual Journalism*, September 19, 2012. https://lens.blogs.nytimes.com/2012/09/19/malcolm-x-as-visual-strategist/
30. Nancy, Jean-Luc. *Noli me Tangere: On the Raising of the Body*. Fordham University Press: 2008.

CHAPTER 3

1. Breitman. *Malcolm X Speaks*. 7.
2. Lipsitz, George. *How Racism Takes Place*. Temple University Press: 2011, 29.
3. Ibid., 55.
4. Breitman. *Malcolm X Speaks*. 35–6.
5. Ibid., 119.
6. Ibid., 42.
7. Foucault, Michel. *Security, Territory, Population: Lectures at the Collège de France 1977–1978*. Picador: 2007, 5.
8. Ibid.
9. Ibid., 4–5.
10. https://en.wikipedia.org/wiki/Power_(physics)
11. https://en.wikipedia.org/wiki/Force
12. Hobsbawm, E. J. *Nations and Nationalism since 1780: Programme, Myth, Reality*. Cambridge: 2006, 8.
13. Special Field Order #15 January 16, 1865.
14. Marable. *Malcolm X*. 361–2.
15. Hegel, G.W. F. *Philosophy of Right*. Cambridge: 1991, 111.
16. Breitman. *Macolm X Speaks*. 50–1.
17. Ibid., 51.
18. Ibid., 52.
19. Marable. *Malcolm X: A Life of Reinvention*, 361–2.

20. Manela, Erez. *The Wilsonian Moment: Self-Determination and the International Origins of Anti-Colonial Nationalism*. Oxford University Press: 2007, 198.

21. Ibid., 22.

22. Campbell, Crystal Z. "Sculpting a Pan-African Culture in the Art of Negritude: A Model for African Artists". *The Journal of Pan-African Studies*, Vol. 1, No. 6, December 2006, 23.

23. Irele, Abiola. "Negritude – Literature and Ideology". *The Journal of Modern African Studies*, Vol. 3, No. 4, December 1965, 499.

24. Skurnik, Walter A.E. "Leopold Sedar Senghor and African Socialism". *The Journal of Modern African Studies*, Vol. 3, No. 3, October 1965, 349.

25. Fanon, Frantz. *Black Skin, White Masks*. Grove Press: 2008, 102.

26. Skurnik. "Leopold Seda Senghor". 367.

CHAPTER 4

1. Breitman. *Malcolm X Speaks*. 47.

2. Ibid., 26.

3. Rancière, Jacques. *Dissensus*. Bloomsbury: 2013, 29.

4. Ibid., 33.

5. Breitman. *Malcolm X Speaks*. 40.

6. Lorde. "The Master's Tools". 94.

7. Breitman. *Malcolm X Speaks*. 28–9.

8. Declaration of Independence. July 4, 1776. Paragraph 3.

9. Breitman. *Malcolm X Speaks*. 49–50.

10. Ibid., 25.

11. Ibid., 34.

12. Ibid., 35.

13. Ibid., 26–7.

14. Ibid., 30.

15. Ibid., 43.

16. Yack, Bernard. *The Longing for Total Revolution: Philosophical Sources of Social Discontent from Rousseau to Marx and Nietzsche*. University of California Press: 1992, 3.

17. Breitman. *Malcolm X Speaks*. 57.

18. Robinson, Cedric. *Black Marxism: The Making of the Black Radical Tradition*. University of North Carolina Press: 1983, 170.

19. Breitman. *Malcolm X Speaks*. 39.

20. Ibid., 199.

21. Fanon. *Wretched of the Earth*. 23.

CONCLUSION

1. www.rimaregas.com/2015/03/01/james-baldwin-on-malcolm-x/

2. Ture, Kwame and Hamilton, Charles V. *Black Power: The Politics of Liberation*. Vintage: 1992, 5.

3. Ibid., 34–5.
4. Ibid., 190.
5. Ibid., xix.
6. Personal communication.
7. www.outkickthecoverage.com/colin-kaepernick-is-an-idiot-082716/
8. https://theundefeated.com/features/colin-kaepernick-mix-of-racism-anti-islam-rhetoric- are-increasingly-toxic/

Index